COMING SOON FROM PIÉRRE RAMON THOMAS

Pink Black Boy: A Memoir in Essays & Poems

THE NOMADIC POET

A COLLECTION OF POETRY & PROSE
PIÉRRE RAMON THOMAS

Revised and reprinted in 2025

The Nomadic Poet: A Collection of Poetry & Prose

Copyright © 2022 Piérre Ramon Thomas. All rights reserved.

No part of this book may be reproduced in any written, electronic, recording, or photocopying without written permission of the author. The exception would be in the case of brief quotations embodied in the critical articles or reviews and pages where permission is specifically granted by the publisher or author.

Introduction Edited by: BookBaby

ISBN: 978-0-9998336-4-3

Library of Congress Control Number: 2021910048

Social Media:
Instagram: @pierreramonthomas
Twitter: @pierrewrites
Email: pierreramonthomas@gmail.com
Website: www.pierreramonthomas.com

Cover Design by: Piérre Ramon Thomas
Artwork by: El'Cesart

TABLE OF CONTENTS

Introduction..v

Author's Note..ix

Fragments of Me

    He Escapes Me..3
    Audacity...4
    Resilient...5
    The Pageant...6
    Conversation with My Teen-Aged Self.........11
    Saboteur..12
    Disappearing Act..13
    Mythical Creature..14
    Man of Vicarious Reconnaissance..................15
    Open Book..16
    The Desecration That Led to the Ruins........17
    Equation..20
    Guarded..21
    Freedom...25

While in the Throes of Emotions

    Cloudy, with Seldom Visits from the Sun.....29
    Numb and Unfazed...30
    My Heart Cracked Open and It Bled.............31
    Love, to Me..33
    Assure Me...35
    Thoughts I Have When the Adversity of Life
            Becomes Too Much............................36
    Nature, Be One with Me...................................37
    Entropy..39

Distrusting Love..40
If I Seem Serious..42
The Day It Shut Down......................................43
Weighed Down..45
Dousing Yet Another Fire................................46
One Second Before Midnight (11:59:59
       p.m.)..47
Pieces..50
Passed Over..51

One Is the Loneliest Number

Inexperienced..55
Why Not Cherish Your Lover?........................56
Open Heart Riddle..58
One of the Few Millennials Tired of Hook-
       Up Culture..59
Foolish..61
Anticipating My Lover.....................................62
In My Final Moments.......................................64
Come Before I Tear...65
Explore My Universe..67
What is Love?..69
On Never Being Able to Keep a Man............71
Small Town, City, Small Town (After Rupi
       Kaur)...72
Haunting Silhouettes..74

If You Will Indulge Me, I Fantasize About Love Too Much

Best Love Story Ever Told...............................79
In It..81
Aspiration...82

You Could Never Love Someone Like Me..83
His Eyes..........87
If I Feel Safe..........89
Between Quivered Breaths..........90
The Consummation..........91
The Army I Formed for You..........94
My Only Desire..........96
Mementos..........98
The Moment..........99
willful exposition..........100
When Forever Is Interrupted..........102
My Government..........103
On Account of You..........105
Is Time Still Time Concerning Us?..........108
Fluent..........110
Our Lovemaking..........111
Escape to Utopia..........115
What I Answer When He Calls..........116
The Swordsmen: The Warrior and the
    Poet..........117
A Profession..........120
Persuading Mr. Self-Sufficient..........124
Gray Hairs..........125
In the Beginning..........127
I Present My Heart to You..........129
Nursed to Health..........131
Allegiance..........133
The Creation of You: A Revelation..........134
The Marionettist..........136
Three Men, Three Diamond Vessels..........137
From Web & Loom..........140
Sometimes the Prey Is the Predator..........141
Street Preacher..........142
A Perfect Argument..........143

I Saw You Before I Met You..........................145
Beau of the Ball...146
More Than a Sexual Creature.........................149
Well Never Empty..150
Perfection Personified....................................151
That Time When We Made Love for
    Forever..153
Spiders & Centipedes.....................................155
The Morning After...156
Poor, but Rich...159
Garlic Spaghetti...161
Past Self < Present Self..................................162
All to Show You My Love.............................163
Love Me in All Elements...............................164
At a Loss for Words.......................................165
If Only You Knew..167
Send This Letter to My Lover, O Bird of the
    Air..169
Blown to Smithereens....................................171
They Say...173
Cause & Effect..175
The Definition of Poetry................................176
Finally..177
Pining Away..179

The Tie That Binds

The Contents of This Wooden Box............183
The Unloved Son...185
The Significance of a Father.........................187
Louis..190
Which Wire Do I Cut?..................................192
A Letter to the Children I May Never
    Have..193

Musings..199 – 212

If They Say Why? Why?–Tell 'Em That It's Human Nature

    The Masked Woman.......................................215
    I Have Yet to See..217
    Give Love Longevity......................................219
    The Hills of Towoldji.....................................220
    Let Words Mean What They Say They
        Mean..223
    Multiplicity Theorem.....................................225
    The Three Hardest Words to Say..................226
    Star-Struck..227
    Light..228
    Processed Food..229
    High Standards..231
    Where Are the Colors in Your Words?........232
    The Romantic Who Doesn't Romanticize
        Love...233
    How Does It Feel to Be God's Favorites?.234
    Be Mindful...236
    Death to Cordiality!......................................237
    I Am Not Psychic But...................................238
    Every Heart Deserves Love..........................239

Poetry About Poetry

    Verbal Orgasms..243
    The Curse of Love Poets...............................244
    Restraining Myself from Poetry...................245
    Out of Words He Created Me......................247
    A Religion Unto Itself..................................249

The Poet's Burden..251

Endnotes..255

DEDICATION

To my grandparents:
Lawrence Sandy Thomas, Sr.
Lovenia Joyce Thomas

Grandda' and Grandma.
Always and forever.

ACKNOWLEDGEMENTS

Thank you El'Cesart for the wonderful artwork.

Follow him on Instagram: @cesar_does_it
To hire him: www.ElCesart.com

Thank you, Dr. Leigh Johnson, associate professor at Marymount University, for your thoughtful feedback on *The Nomadic Poet*. I am humbled by your words and am forever in your debt.

INTRODUCTION

Although the word *nomad* means 'a wanderer; an individual who roams about', I ask that you, the reader, will give me just a little flexibility, *poetic* license, if you will, in the application of the word. *I am a nomadic poet.* I am a nomadic poet because, as you will witness in the forthcoming pages, the subject matter of my literature tends to deviate from the norm.

The general consensus says that art should be reflective of the times, but I contend that there should be room for art to be transportive, whimsical, and fantastical. I am not arguing that all art should be given to imagination—human rights issues and environmental justice are buttressed by art. For example, I owe much of my environmentalism to shows like *Captain Planet*. My "no littering" principle was inspired by its theme song:

> *Captain Planet*
> *He's our hero*
> *Gonna take pollution down to zero*

...

> *We're the planeteers,*
> *You can be one too!*
> *'Cause saving our planet is the thing to do,*
> *Looting and polluting is not the way,*
> *Hear what Captain Planet has to say:*

"THE POWER IS YOURS!"

It was Smokey the Bear, a cartoon commercial mascot, who told me that only I could prevent wildfires. NBC's *Superstore* comically addressed issues like racism, maternal leave, and universal healthcare in a non-corny, non-ham-handed way. Clearly, I believe that art should be reflective of the times—but sometimes. Not all art *has to be* reflective, or should be. That's where *The Nomadic Poet* comes in. With police brutality diseasing America, the Earth burning, and human rights violations happening in places like Uganda, I believe, sometimes, for the sake of our mental health, we need a temporary escape via film and literature. I have written and collated these compositions so that you may be transported, for a brief moment, to my fantastical, deeply emotive, ethereal world. That you may journey to another realm and find reprieve. At least until we snap back to reality and we deal with difficult matters again. But the option should be available, especially in literature, for one to escape.

I've noticed that black people have been artistically pigeonholed. From my point of view, it seems that it is mostly black people who create visual art, literary art, or performative art about race and racism. In order for us to be recognized for our works or talents, the central theme of our narratives *has to be* related to race and racism in some way. I want to have the privilege that white people have and be able to create literature unrelated to race/racism. I realize that by bringing this matter up in the Introduction, I run the risk of pigeonholing myself. However, I bring it up in case someone wonders why I, a black person, am not talking about racism, microaggressions, gentrification, and police brutality. Talking about race and racism is not the only concern of black people;

black people have many other interests: love, joy, family, religion or spirituality, and so many other topics regarding human nature. I should be able to create literature that is a form of escapism from the maddening reality of America. I should be able to take a mental health break from thinking about Tamir Rice, Breonna Taylor, Eric Garner, and their families (although I constantly think about them outside of my literature). I should be able to forget that there are uniformed men and women who assume that my blackness is an immediate threat, who will not hesitate to use lethal force if I so much as flinch or twitch my nose. I should be able to not think about the fact that an unarmed black person will be treated with deadlier force than an armed white person—(and before racists say anything, I'd like to tell them that there is ample video evidence of this happening).

As a black poet, I realize that my literature may never be received like that of r.h. Sin, Rudy Francisco, or Pierre Alex Jeanty, because of my sexuality. I am a man who desires and enjoys the company of men. The subjects or love interests of my love poems are men. (Though I do sometimes make faithful efforts to keep the subjects of my compositions ambiguous so that all may be able to enjoy and identify with my poetry). You will not find love poems to women within these pages. And as a black, *gay* poet, I have made peace with the fact that my compositions may not be received like those of Danez Smith, Donte Collins or Jericho Brown. Their literature is reflective of our times, whereas my head is off in the clouds somewhere. Those poets are talking about relevant issues while I'm off composing romantic fantasies or baring my soul, talking about things like loneliness. Reader, please don't take this as me trying to garner sympathy for myself. Let me ask you: Have you ever had something that burned hot in you? Singing? Painting? Acting? Dancing? Cooking? Did it burn so fervently in your chest that you felt like if you didn't do it, if you didn't act out your passions, that you just might die? I may seem melodramatic but that's what writing is for me. That's what *The Nomadic Poet* is for me. So even at the risk of no one ever reading this, I write to get the fire out. I write to cool down. I write even though I know I may not be named among the r.h. Sins, Rudy Franciscos, Pierre Alex Jeantys, Danez Smiths, Donte Collinses or the Jericho Browns of the world. And this is okay with me.

  Nomadic poets have a tendency to write according to the content of their own, individual poetic spirits. Nomadic poets might create some literary art that supports whatever literary movement that's *en vogue* during their writing career (probably because they need to stand out among the hundreds of thousands of poets and want to make a name for themselves), but, for the most part, their literature will be different, distinct, and unique to them. The topics and themes of the poetry of nomadic poets aren't different because they aim to be literary contrarians going against the *status quo* just to be edgy or rebellious. The topics and themes of their poetry are different because they've made a conscious choice to write according to what their poetic spirits want to say. Nothing more, nothing less.

Author's Note

Sometimes, I speak in symbols. (Symbolism is not exclusive to my literature). It will do me no good if you, the reader, don't understand my symbolism. In some of the compositions, there are annotations, numbered annotations which correspond with the Endnotes. In many cases, symbols that I use in some pieces can be referenced in other pieces. The whole of my poetry and prose is an ecosystem of its own; my compositions may be individually titled and individually composed, but they relate to one another.

Lastly, I understand that Instagram poetry and micropoetry are the flavor *du jour*. No disrespect to those writers but that isn't the type of poetry I write. However, I recognize that in our busy lives, we don't have time for lengthy discourses or Odyssean-like poems. Please feel free to take your time while you leaf through these pages. I recommend a bookmark so that my sometimes-long poetry or prose don't keep you from the more significant matters in your life. Indulge, but pace yourself.

FRAGMENTS OF ME

He Escapes Me

I see very distinctly in my mind's eye
The reflection of a man gentler, more
    serene than I.
The man I see is me, yet he's also not
    me,
For he's who I'm not, but he who I
    aim to be.
I can almost apprehend him, he whose
    nature is petal-like soft
But he escapes my grasp, perches the
    nearest cloud aloft.
He runs from him whose composition
    is jagged, scraggly stone,
From him whose tempests never end,

From him on whom it seems light has
    never shone.

Piérre Ramon Thomas

Audacity

The hills embolden me.
For if they can arc as high as they do
And expand farther than the eye can
    measure,
Then so can I.

Resilient

I thought my troubles would break me,
    Yet, I am whole still.

I thought my anguish would end me,
    Yet, I continue still.

I thought my pains would do me in,
    Yet, I do outstanding still.

I thought my sorrows would undo me,
    Yet, I am together still.

I thought my grief would kill me,
    Yet, I live still.

Piérre Ramon Thomas

The Pageant

(A Fable)

They lined us all up in four rows of
    twenty-five.
There I stood, a contestant,
About to be judged on the beauty of
    my face among a host of
Stunningly
    Gorgeous
        Men.
Standing beside me were the likes of:
Adam Rippon,
Jason Carter,
Keiynan Lonsdale,
And Bretman Rock.
Each one of them stepped forward as
    the judges held up numbered
    cards;
The audience roared, cheering for
    their favorite,
               Shaking the auditorium.
When I stepped forward, the judges,
    unimpressed,
Each held up a card with a zero.
The cricket in the audience was the
    only one who cheered for me.

Still, I kept my head held high
And my smile did not falter.

The Nomadic Poet

They lined us all up in four rows of
    twenty-five.
There I stood, a contestant,
About to be judged on the
    musculature of my body among a
    line-up of
Perfectly
    Chiseled
        Beefcakes.
Standing beside me were the likes of:
Jason Momoa,
Joe Manganiello,
Dwayne "The Rock" Johnson,
And Michael B. Jordan.
Each one of them stepped forward as
    the judges held up numbered
    cards;
The audience whooped and hollered
    for their favorite
             Losing their sanity.
When I stepped forward, the judges,
    rolling their eyes,
Each held up a card with a zero.
The cricket in the crowd was the only
    one who whooped and hollered
    for me.

Still, I kept my head held high
And my smile did not falter.

They lined us all up in four rows of
    twenty-five.
There I stood, a contestant,

Piérre Ramon Thomas

About to be judged on my overall
    style and fashion among a mob of
Avant-garde,
    Chic
        Fashion Icons.
Walking the catwalk with me were the
    likes of:
Neil Patrick Harris,
Tim Gunn,
André Leon Talley,
And Colman Domingo.
Each one of them walked the runway
    while the judges held up
    numbered cards;
The audience clapped, *oohing* and
    aahing at each outfit,
        Sounding like a choir.
When I walked the runway, the
    judges, pursing their lips,
Each help up a card with a zero.
The cricket was the only one in the
    room who *oohed* and *aahed* at me.

Still, I kept my head held high
And my smile did not falter.

They lined us all up in four rows of
    twenty-five.
There I stood, a contestant,
About to be judged on the skill of my
    poetry among a roster of
Heavyweight
    Writing
        Juggernauts.

The Nomadic Poet

Standing beside me were the likes of:
Ocean Vuong,
Rudy Francisco,
Sabrina Benaim,
And Danez Smith.
Each one of them recited poems and
    afterwards, the judges held up
    numbered cards;
The audience wolf-whistled, rooting
    for their favorite
        Filling the corners of the auditorium
            with their noise.
When I finished my recitations, the
    judges, faces deadpanned,
Each held up a card with a zero.
The cricket, unable to wolf-whistle,
    chirped his loudest for me.

Still, I kept my head held high
And my smile did not falter.

At the end of the pageant,
Each Beautiful Boy was given a
    bouquet of freshly cut red roses,
Each Muscle Man was awarded a sash
    around his shoulder,
Each Style Icon was honored with a
    glass trophy,
Each Skillful Poet was decorated with
    medals placed over their necks,
All except me.

Backstage,

Piérre Ramon Thomas

I genuinely congratulated each
   contestant, shaking their hands.

Still, I kept my head held high
And my smile did not falter.

To my surprise,
The cricket found me afterwards
And gave me a plucked petal from a
   red rose.
He said, "If only I could carry more,
I would've brought you a bouquet's
   worth."
I bent down, scooped him up,
And placed him on my shoulder.
He leaned over and whispered to me,
"Even if no one on this Earth
Loves you,
Appreciates you,
Or cheers for you,
Do so for yourself."
As tears skated down my cheeks,
I could do nothing but respond with a
   smile.

I kept my head held high
And my smile did not falter.

The Nomadic Poet

Conversation with My Teen-Aged Self

If I had the opportunity to meet my
　　younger self,
There wouldn't be much
　　conversation.
I would take that violent whirlwind of
　　hurt, pain, and anger
Enclose him in my arms as long as
　　was necessary until the storm
　　calmed.
I would collect the tears he would
　　inevitably cry
Go and water the wildfires in
　　California.
I would soothe his unsettled soul with
　　the whispers, "I know. I know."
For no other words but those
Could quell the unrest inside him.
Before disappearing into thin air,
I would leave him with these parting
　　words:
"Hold on to what I say. You are
　　greatly loved, young one.

　　　YOU ARE LOVED."

Piérre Ramon Thomas

Saboteur

(A Soliloquy)

Saboteur,
Why won't you stop sabotaging me?
You will not be satisfied until I am left
    destitute.
I take one step forward,
You send me three steps back;
I climb up to the zenith,
You knock me down to the ground.
You are the reason I can't progress;
On account of you, I go around in
    circles.
I must reestablish every component
Every time you tear down my work.

Ancestors, save me!
Save me please from *this saboteur*.

Disappearing Act

I am not a magician,
But before people take my presence
    for granted
And not appreciate its gift,
I vanish,
Leaving not even a lingering whiff of
    my fragrance.
Stupefied, they look all around
    themselves,
Wondering where I went
And why.

Piérre Ramon Thomas

Mythical Creature

Flowers emerge from the earth wherever he strides,
Greenery becomes greener with his presence;
His robe of clouds explains why it appears he glides
On unfettered air which is his essence.
It is clear that *pink* is his language of choice,
He revels in his unique color;
Some men despise the flamboyancy of his voice,
Grumble and complain it should be duller.
He tosses handfuls of glitter dramatically in the air,
Glitter that resembles his crown of stars;
To happen upon another like him is rare
For the traits of boldness and confidence are sparse.

The Nomadic Poet

Man of Vicarious Reconnaissance

I evade
Unpleasant situations
Similar to others
Because
I witness
Their catastrophe
And avoid
Their footsteps.

Piérre Ramon Thomas

Open Book

I am your table of contents and your
    preface,
Your glossary and your index;
If you are curious to know me or
    about me,
Simply crack open my spine and trace
    your fingers along the words on
    the pages—
Or in other words—
Simply ask me.

The Desecration That Led to the Ruins

(A Poetic Tale)

A holy temple of love it was supposed
    to be;
A consecrated monastery for one
    dedicated monk its initial purpose.

Having separate butterfly and bird
    sanctuaries,
Complete with a rose garden whose
    glory fully expressed in spring.

Celibate stonemasons constructed the
    sacred edifice meticulously by
    hand;
Virginal seamstresses sewn elaborate
    fabrics for the inner sanctum.

This romantic church[1] had granite
    fountains in its courtyard,
Bronze statues and ornate topiaries
    led passersby to the entrance.

Plush, teal carpets lined the floor of
    the sanctuary,
Mahogany wood was cut and
    fashioned into pews.
The Architect[2] drew up a special
    bedroom to house the high
    priest[3]—

Piérre Ramon Thomas

A special place, deep in the heart of
 the temple,
A place for his rest and relaxation.

The entire temple was constructed for
 a high priest:
A man so knowledgeable in the art of
 love
His wisdom would serve as an
 example for laypeople.[4]
The plan was for the high priest to
 teach visiting priests,[5]
How they were supposed to mind
 their temples.

However,

The temple-keeper[6] allowed
 undesirable men into the temple,
Sacrilegious hooligans tracked mud on
 the carpet, dripped blood from
 their previous victims.
Bombarding through the holy place,
 they stole sanctified goldwares
 meant for worship,
What they could not steal, they
 desecrated with profane graffiti or
 destroyed with clubs and torches.

Foolishly, the temple-keeper thought
 the men would be harmless,
He presumed the men would visit the
 monastery and either stay

temporarily or one would become a priest himself.
Outnumbered by the mob of careless gangsters,[7]
The temple-keeper ran to the nearest forest, fell to the ground wailing, and intensely prayed for death.

After some time, the temple-keeper returned to assess what had become of the formerly splendid structure,
To his dismay, what he found was rubble, overturned statues, and perpetual smoke rising from the ruins.[8]
With the atom of strength that remained in his helpless, sorrowful soul,
He did the best he could to restore it to its former glory.

Piérre Ramon Thomas

Equation

Although I am the mathematician's
    frustration,
Diligence pays off.

Every advanced equation,
Every complex mathematical problem
Has a solution.

Guarded

Guarded:
> When people expect a caricature, a stereotype, a carbon copy, something comfortable and familiar instead of my unconventional, individualistic self.

Guarded:
> When people expect the worst from me because they've never experienced someone like me. I've had *multiple* people tell me that they first expected me to be characteristic of all the worst stereotypes of black and/or gay people, but were surprised at how *"different"* I am.

Guarded:
> Because people don't know how to receive me. Instead of being experts in the art of allowing a person to unfold before them and accepting people as they present themselves, I've often been compared or held up to previous models, preconceived notions, or generalizations. I've been called "fake nice" (because people are not used to my brand of politeness). I've had people tell me, "You're not a *regular* gay guy" or, "You're not like *typical* gay guys". I've had people tell me, "You know you B*lack*, right?"

Guarded:

When human beings can't be humane to one another because they're inhumane monsters.

Guarded:
When people get attitudes and complain that I don't speak, but they have mouths that can speak as well—*but don't*—but they're the only ones complaining about someone not speaking.

Guarded:
My mother used to lock herself in her room for days on end and we weren't allowed to bother her. But people expect me to be like an open field. Many have been offended because this gay man isn't a social butterfly.

Guarded:
When I do open myself up, the rare instances that I do, people trip over themselves to be hurtful and careless and reckless with my feelings. Hurt is bound to come because we're humans, but it's what that human does *after* being hurtful that matters.

Guarded:
Because being cautious with the people who I allow in my life has been beneficial for my privacy, as well as my mental health.

Guarded:
When people expect me to be conceited because of the way that I look. When they assume that I think

that I'm better than others. When, knowing nothing of me nor engaging me in conversation, presume that I will be narcissistic, a bitch, stuck-up, or a mean boy.

Guarded:
Because people will look for anything—*anything*—to trash you and badmouth you and drag your name through the mud. They foam at the mouth for every opportunity to curse your name rather than not have your name in their mouth at all.

Guarded:
Because I've been hurt before. Naturally, people try to do everything they can to prevent being hurt again.

Unguarded: When people don't expect me to be a caricature; they embrace me as I am.

Unguarded: When people accept *all* of me. My strengths and my weaknesses. My positive traits and my flaws. My complexities. My intricacies. My quirks. My oddities. My unconventionalities.

Unguarded: When people show humanity—not just to me but to *all* the poor, the disenfranchised, and to service workers from *every* industry.

Unguarded: When people don't get caught up in who speaks first, whether it's me or them. When people understand that it takes time for a person to open up.

Unguarded: When people make mistakes but are evolved enough to be reflective and apologize or, apologize when a wrong is brought to their attention.

Unguarded: When people can acknowledge and compliment me on my accomplishments, successes, and good qualities because they're not insecure, intimidated, and they didn't erroneously conclude that I can't take a compliment because, according to them, "it'll go to my head" or they don't want to "gas me up".

Unguarded: When people are able to call me out on my mistakes, failures, and flaws because they love me and desire to see me be the best version of myself.

Letting my guard down:
As I am learning to trust again.

Freedom

Outdoors resonates with my soul
Because I long to be free like nature.
It is my ambition one day,
To break free from the concrete-and-
    asphalt prison,
Discover my liberty in the soil.
When that time comes,
I, like an Olympian runner,
Will run from the menacingly serious,
    stoic man:
The one with the furrowed brow and
    crossed arms,
        The one whose name is *City*;
Until I happen upon the naked
    woman:
She who sprawls herself out,
Whose breasts greet the heavens,
        The one whose name is *Nature*.

WHILE IN THE THROES OF EMOTIONS

Cloudy, with Seldom Visits from the Sun

The field that has long stood cold,[9]
In mercy is warmed whenever the
    sun[10] touches her with his heat.
The overcast[11] from clouds,
Daily keeps the sun from being
    affectionate to frigid, stiff earth.[12]

Piérre Ramon Thomas

Numb and Unfazed

Vibrations from the mere sound of thunder
Used to scare me, and would invoke the fear of God,
But since I am filled with unending sadness, carrying immeasurable anger,
I don't even flinch anymore I am so numb.

My Heart Cracked Open and It Bled

My heart cracked open and it bled,
And the red flow trickled down
From my home,
Through the streets,
In the grass,
And into the woods.
And my mind was left suspended in
    mid-air.
No one constricted my mouth,
I became mute.
And I wasn't blind,
My eyes just didn't see anyone.
Eventually, the quiet became quiet,
And my movement didn't have a
    sound.
To that specific opinion,
I became a prisoner.
It was by knowledge that I had
    escaped.
It was like being frozen in thick ice,
Then I was thawed.
I thought to myself,
'If only someone had caught me
While I was falling,
Maybe I wouldn't have attacked the ground
    with my body,
The way that I did.'

No visitors where I reside,
Only bypassing spectators.

Piérre Ramon Thomas

My heart cracked open and it bled.
And a little girl pointed at me
And said,
"Mommy! He looks like the porcelain
     doll I dropped,
Broken.
You know. The one you gave me."
At that, my eyes watered the soil,
Only to get back to tending my yard.

My heart cracked open and it bled.
That's why my sheets are red.
That's why my clothes are stained
And you hear the *slosh slosh* sound in
     my shoes.

When my heart cracked open,
Right after the blood started pouring,
Misery crept through the slit
Just to taunt this once all-together
     piece.
How does one evict such a company
And prevent it from returning
If the gap is not patched up?

The blood was cascading
Because the heart was cracked open
Because the young man was picked up
And dropped.

Love, to Me

(Ekphrastic. Inspired by "My Last Duchess" by Robert Browning. The painting referred to: *Ask Me No More*, 1906 by Sir Lawrence Alma-Tadema [Digital Copy]. Also inspired by "Song for a Rainy Day" by Angela Bofill)

Ask me not how I came
    Upon *Ask Me No More*,
The account of which, a true tale,
    Would spend you to your core.

Alma-Tadema actually depicts
    A love that can never be,
But, unbeknownst to him, he foredrew
    The sentiment: *lovelorn me*.

How much does the bowing gentleman
    Represent romantic poverty;
His neck: the straightest line ever drawn
    In geometry!

So thoroughly does he stoop and bend,
    So deep and emphatically;
Kissing her hand, gifting her flowers,
    Begging the lady his eternally.

But the woman doesn't deign the poor man
    A mere millimeter of attention,
One could assume her heart never his for the
        taking—
    A cruel, coldhearted intention!

Piérre Ramon Thomas

Her small, white digits couldn't slip
    From his lips fast enough;
The looming clouds in the horizon ominous
    Of a heart soon faring rough.

I, now, am *Lovepoor*.
    Address me no more by that French name;
Love, to me currently,
    Is that fleeting, blushing dame.

Before the red carnation
    Falls from my ear,
Love raises the leg for departure,
    With feelings nonchalant and cavalier.

Assure Me

Your eyes are everywhere else
Except upon what's beside you.
Instead of admiring someone's beauty,
You are committing infidelity without
 intercourse.
Without a word or gesture,
You engage your body language to
 play along with your stares.
Instead of making me feel like I am
 the prettiest man,
I have to compete with the thinnest
 and the most masculine,
The youngest and the most muscular.
I, on the other hand, do not have
 adulterating eyes;
When I am with you, my focus is
 solely on you.
When we are out together,
Make me feel like the only man on
 Earth with you.
Noting beauty is one thing,
Flirting and desiring another is
 another thing altogether.
If at any time you feel you need to
 chase your fantasies,
Inform me and let me go.
I'd rather have the decency of your
 fidelity
Than the harshness of your uncaring
 heart.

Piérre Ramon Thomas

Thoughts I Have When the Adversity of Life Becomes Too Much

Sometimes I wish God would make
Me weightless enough to glide
Upon the chariot of the wind and let it
    take
Me to a cave somewhere to hide,
Far away from the cruel, uncaring
    ways
Of life's stonyhearted callousness;
I count seconds, minutes, hours, days,
For rescue from this sorrowful abyss.

What benefit is life to man
If he suffers each day he lives?
Would not death be better than
The quality of life life gives?

Life is sprinkled here and there
With just enough good to distract
Us from the problem that life is so
    unfair:
Opens its mouth, swallows us, before
    we can react.

Nature, Be One with Me

Yesterday it rained.
This time I wasn't dissatisfied;
Usually I love sunny days and clear
   nights,
But the somber sight matched how I
   felt inside.
During the day the sky was gray,
The sun kept trying to peer through;
When the sky returned to its saddened
   state,
My soul bonded with the view.
I was crying on the inside
Just as nature had done;
The raindrops heavily dropped
   periodically,
Nature and I were one.
Sometimes my floods are heavy,
At other times, my creeks are silent;
When my emotions become
   overwhelming,
Then my tsunamis[13] soon turn violent.
When it thunders, O God, make the
   heavens shake,
So severely my body starts to quiver;
Let the lightening crack and slice
   through trees—
God, I know you can deliver.
Nature, be one with me,
It is wonderful how you can express,
All the agony that lies in my heart,

Piérre Ramon Thomas

The pain and the distress.
I wanted to weep yesterday
Until my tear ducts were dry,
But nature did it for me,
It said, "I'll be the one to cry."
When the winds rush through the
    trees
Causing them to move wildly,
Let my anger fuel their force,
Let their sounds lift my voice ever so
    loudly.
Nature, be one with me.
Display emotion the way I should;
Articulate for this unlearned man
Until I am just as good.

Entropy

I could gamble any money that I ever
    touched—or ever will touch,
That you have never prayed for
    entropy.

Have you?
Have you ever prayed for entropy?
Have you ever prayed that you would
    fall to pieces,
Prayed that you would split perfectly
    in two,
All because you and the sweetness of
    life were strangers,
Or maybe
The sweetness of life has made an
    enemy of you?

I have.
I have wailed before,
Willing all of the cells in the universe
    of my body,
To give up their occupation,
And let me tend towards degradation,
If it meant that death was hastened,
Putting me out of my misery,
Bringing the sweet relief that I
    severely needed.

Piérre Ramon Thomas

Distrusting Love

Like boiling water thrown on the skin,
Like a long, sharp pin thrusted
    through the body,
So is the pain of rejection.
I have developed, for myself, a shell
    made of metal;
I have built up a thick wall of stone
    around me—
No one will penetrate and mistreat
    this heart.
I just don't understand:
Some treat the heart as if it was *made*
    to be roughed up,
Not seeing that, when it's wholly
    given and widely open,
The heart is a fragile, tender piece;
If mishandled,
It could bring devastation to innocent
    bystanders.

Why should I make the next love
    affair difficult
If he didn't contribute to the hurt and
    pain I carry?
Why should he have to wrap
    mountains in silk cloths
And pour the ocean in crystal vessels
And build a gazebo for the sun and
    moon to enjoy

The Nomadic Poet

And select the brightest stars from the
    sky to clothe me with
All to prove his love for me?

My body complains because I must
    make the next one wait for
    intimacy
Because I must be assured that he is
    with me *for me*.
It's painful to see my trust slow to
    develop
If the next one seems trustworthy—
    and proves it time after time.

Piérre Ramon Thomas

If I Seem Serious

(A Lamentation)

The sky has become iron,
The soil has hardened itself;
My prayers are birds with broken
    wings,
The earth refuses to receive me.

My tears are puddles on the asphalt,
My sorrow is God's Friday night
    entertainment;
It has rained incessantly for a decade
    now,
And I star in a movie with no end.

Clouds alone share my grief,
Windchill reflects iciness in my heart;
If anyone needs water, my eyes are a
    fountain,
Callous misdeeds have robbed me of
    my warmth.

Loneliness is my last remaining friend,
Silence, a tried-and-true comforter;
The only company I receive is my
    involuntary solitude,
The solace I get comes from the
    nothingness of the empty void.

The Day It Shut Down

I'm surprised you didn't hear about it,
And there were no articles printed in
    newspapers or magazines.
I honestly thought the town would be
    ringing,
With news of its closing.

The doors slammed shut...
Wait... *Yes! I remember the date!*
It was August the 6th, 2012.
Mark the date on your calendars,
For a memorial must be given,
It deserves, at least, that much.
The whirring of the machines faded
    and died,
The drapes were extended,
The electricity was cut off,
And all the factory workers were laid
    off and sent home.

The mourners of the town stood
    nearby,
Wailing at its misfortune—
I joined them.
The mourners of town lifted up their
    voices,
And all the townspeople heard.

As I watched all of this, I learned
    something:

Piérre Ramon Thomas

If another is shut down,
I must stop,
Take notice,
And sympathize.
For if too many are shut down,
The world would lose its luminance.

There *is* hope, however.
The building[14] is not closed
    permanently.

Weighed Down

As of late, I have been jealous of the wind, For it, Being unburdened and light, Flows, drifts, breezes wherever it pleases. Contrarily, I am weighed down, Restricted to one place; Forbidden from riding air currents to Far off spaces Because of my troubles: The things that vex me.

Piérre Ramon Thomas

Dousing Yet Another Fire

Why did you arrange the stones in a
　　circle,
Gather firewood of oak and pine,
With flint and steel ignite a fire,[15]
And prolong the flames with tinder
　　and kindling

Only to abandon the hungry inferno
Leaving it to roar vigorously towards
　　the sky,
Leaving it to wax and wane in want
For you to immolate yourself?

You ought to know that it hurts,
Painful to extinguish yet another fire,
The type that has been lit time and
　　time again
By men, *proud pyromaniacs*,
Who left it[16] blazing:
Crackling hopefulness[17] in the
　　beginning,
Then burning self-pity[18] in the end.

One Second Before Midnight (11:59:59 p.m.)[19]

(An Apostrophe. First published in Marymount University's 2021 Literary Arts Magazine *BlueInk*)

Philosophy,
I meant not such a predicament for
    you.
Shrouded is the face that once smiled
    upon a fool;
In burlap they smother you.
The knowledgeable head that fed me
    things better than food,
Now lying upon a guillotine;
The hands that once clothed me in the
    garments of scholars,
Suffer rope burns on their wrists.

Spirituality,
Never did I foresee trouble for you.
The white and gold apparel in which
    you were donned,
Is bunched on the ground, tattered,
    torn, discolored by dirt;
In iron they shackle you, your wrists
    and ankles,
Stretching you out like they aim to
    rend your appendages.
Gashes from the lashes of the whip
    mark your body,
Your shrieks imprint the same inside
    my appalled soul.

Piérre Ramon Thomas

Human Nature,
Far was it from me that you would
    suffer such sick sorrows.
It wasn't enough for them to starve
    you
Until you were bones-pronounced
    gaunt,
Satisfied they weren't keeping you in
    the dark, in God-forsaken
    solitude,
Deprived of the warmth of the sun or
    that of another creature;
In a cauldron of water they have set
    you,
And, without a modicum of sympathy,
    they have lit the wood.

Love, my most cherished muse[20] of
    all,
How I wish you and your fellows
    remained unharmed from ever
    knowing me!
Black eyes and cut lips your beautiful
    face displays,
As a result from the punches and
    kicks they issued.
That frame of yours that once stood
    tall and erect, with a steel-hard
    spine,
Has collapsed about the pavement like
    a demolished building.
Over your heart the enemy has
    hoisted his sword,

The Nomadic Poet

The lip of his blade gleaming with
    thirst of your flesh.

God, if not for the sake of me,
For them, please, I pray:
Help me free them;
They should not suffer on account of
    me.[21]
If ever You loved me,
If ever I meant anything to You,
You would rescue them from the grip
    of my enemies,
Let me take their place instead.

Piérre Ramon Thomas

Pieces

Some days,
I am pieced together nicely.
Other days,
I am in shambles, puzzle pieces strewn across the floor.
On those days,
I am responsible for picking up the fragments of myself,
And fitting them back together.

Many days—
Even while I was reduced to bits and shards myself—
I was relied upon to be a master ceramicist
To many a sad and broken hearts.

It would be nice though—
Even once—
To rely on someone else to glue together this porcelain
When it has been violently smashed to a thousand pieces.

Passed Over

I am a poem left unread.
I am poetry left unsaid.
I am a painting to the blind.
I am a sculpture patrons don't mind.
I am a song sung to an empty room.
I am a singer who sings to the moon.
I am an instrument not played.
I am an orchestra spitefully delayed.

I am a train's horn in the distance,
Riding through town, soon gone, for
    instance.
I am a robin in the youth of morn,
Encouraged by early laborers yet the
    sleepers' scorn.

I am a book not bought.
I am knowledge not taught.
I am wisdom unsought.

I am gold in the earth,
Unbothered,
And unwrought.

ONE IS THE LONELIEST NUMBER

Inexperienced

No,
I have not found the clean, cerulean
    sky.
I have not laid eyes upon the moon
    giving one last exhibition
Of her beauty before she retires for
    the night.
I have not been greeted by the breeze
    of the wind
Dancing around me with the grace of
    a ballerino.
Birds chirping in the faded distance is
    a sound I have not heard
Nor the liveliness of schoolchildren
    playing, waiting for their school
    bus.
I have not seen grass coated in
    morning dew.
A ladybug has not explored the
    vastness of my hand.
I have not been draped with the finest
    pieces of thread;
Silk is a fabric that I do not know.
I have not looked out into nature and
    saw God,
The existence of Him in every leaf or
    the scurry of a random squirrel.

But I am hoping to.

Piérre Ramon Thomas

Why Not Cherish Your Lover?

How is it that *I* am to walk this road
    of life alone
While others, who treat love like a
    joke,
Have an assortment of lovers?
I have to go without a companion
While the next person handles their
    treasure carelessly.
The fourteenth of February is not
    Lover's Day for me,
It is a day when my loneliness and
    sorrow is made loud and clear.
I always ask myself,
Why is it agonizing to see lovebirds
    kissing and hugging?
It is because I have no lips to meet
And I have no arms surrounding me.
I know I shouldn't feel the ungrateful
    lover doesn't deserve their mate,
It's just if I had a confidant I would
    cherish him.
If I found someone who deserved me,
I would take care of him.

I would say,
"Don't worry about your supper;
I'll prepare it for you.
Don't worry about your body;
I'll wash it for you.
No need for a therapist;

The Nomadic Poet

I'll be your listener.
What are your dreams?
I'll put my faith in you.
What are your fears?
I'll shield you.
What are your sorrows?
Share them with me and I'll weep with
    you.
What are your joys?
I'll laugh and celebrate with you."

There are some who don't appreciate
    their lover.
There are some who mislead their
    mate and care not for the other's
    heart.
I still wonder how they could have
    someone,
When someone like me remains alone.

Piérre Ramon Thomas

Open Heart Riddle

Riddle me this:
How can one keep himself guarded to
 prevent getting hurt,
And at the same time keep his heart
 vulnerable
So that he is not standoffish?

If only love was regarded sacred,
There would be no Great Wall of
 China;
If only the heart was considered
 porcelain,
There would be no Antarctica.

The Nomadic Poet

One of the Few Millennials Tired of Hook-Up Culture

No more do I want to bed-hop[22] or
    have bed-hoppers;[23]
The next one who sexes me has to
    first befriend me.
He has to captivate my mind and
    heart—
My complete interest—
Before he can conquer my body.
My thoughts about him must be so
    abundant
That I forget what frowns are.
My heart must melt at the memory of
    his touches and kisses,
My mind must stay preoccupied with
    ideas of how to keep him pleased
Before I give myself fully.

What a heartache it is when you invest
    all of your emotions and feelings,
Your time and your body,
Into one who does not reciprocate the
    same,
Into one who should not receive those
    precious things.

Here I am,
Standing in the Courting Field,[24]
With my heart and mind and
    sensuality in a basket,

Piérre Ramon Thomas

Waiting to give it to the one who has shown me he is worth entrusting myself to.

Foolish

I have tried to not want love,
Assuming not wanting love
Would ease the pain of not being
    desired,
Sparing me from the torture of living
    life alone.

But...no matter how many times I try,
I always come to the realization:
It is not sustainable to not want love;
A heart is no good to anyone if it is
    numb.

Piérre Ramon Thomas

Anticipating My Lover

When will my lover come?
How long must I wait?
Will I have to be at my second to last
 breath
Before I lay eyes upon his face?
It's easy to say, "Have patience,"
When romance is surrounding you.
So, no more trying to pacify me with
 empty words dear friend,
Since I have not yet seized my lover.

Have my setting in the middle of the
 ocean
Where I'll be in desperate need of
 land.
Have my setting in the middle of the
 desert
Where my tongue will need water.
But please do not set me in this world
Needing a loving spirit to keep me
 company.

I wondered, *'Is there something wrong with
 me?'*
Then I remembered, *'No, wait a minute!
 I am flawed perfection.'*

Then I cry:
Make haste, make haste my love.

Come to me but leave not your heart
   behind.
Carry a fire in you
And set me afire with your passions.
Let us move from lust to another
   dimension undiscovered,
Where the meeting of our souls is
   more important than the meeting
   of our bodies.
I desire to move beyond my fantasies
For they anger me 'cause I cannot
   touch that which I dream.

Why must Time[25] torture me and
   Reality[26] tease me?
They say, "Your lover has not yet
   come.
Silly dreamer!
You will depart from this world not
   knowing the adoration of
   another."

Piérre Ramon Thomas

In My Final Moments

When I stare into the barrel of the gun
    of death
And see its bullet waiting for me,
Itching to propel forward and pierce
    my flesh,
I realize that
In my final moments,
When time comes for Death Angel to
    snipe me,
I'd rather go out surrounded by the
    love and laughter of *one* soul with
    whom I have a shared history
Than emptiness, loneliness, and a long
    list of a slew of bodies that I knew
    at some point or other.

Come Before I Tear

Baring my soul, I admit:
Earnestly I crave to be with someone.
This solitary walk is growing old;
It is time for my lover to make an
    entrance.
I have tried to tarry
But I have grown anxious;
I am like the alcoholic
    without his drink
Or the addict
    without his fix.
My whole bodily system has become
    hungry,
For a romantic interaction,
For a joining of souls.
If my wait is any longer,
I do believe I will tear to many pieces,
My fortress would freeze over,
And my heart would slip into a frozen
    paralysis.
The tears I cry,
Would flow into the Atlantic Ocean.
For me, it would be a perpetual
    nightfall,
The moon would hide her face from
    me,
And sob at my misfortune.
Sadly, I would continue to experience
    love
Through love ballads

Piérre Ramon Thomas

And observing other couples'
moments of affection.

Explore My Universe

Is there not *one* left on Earth
Who has met NASA prerequisites to
 become an astronaut,
One who possesses an unquenchable
 thirst
To explore the extents of another's
 universe?

Does not *one* exist who finds the stars
 surrounding me exquisite enough
To venture through the glittering
 lights on an odyssey of
 exploration?
Is there not *one* who regards stargazing
 insufficient for him
And therefore braves the journey
 through the constellations until he
 knows every star by name?

Is there not *one* studious astronomer
Who desires to understand the
 phenomenon of solar flares?[27]
Is there not *one* soul courageous
 enough to orbit the burning sun[28]
Until he is able to colonize the Titan
 Star[29] due to the thoroughness of
 his own passion?

Piérre Ramon Thomas

Does not *one* exist who finds the gravity of lovelessness or false love[30] on Earth cumbersome
That he desires to know what the weightlessness of interstellar space[31] feels like?
Is there not *one* adventurous enough to board whatever spacecraft he has
On a life-long mission unlike anything he has ever experienced?

What Is Love?

What is love
If sickness can rend my heart,
The object of my affection,
From the center of my bosom?

What is love if my world can end
Because death has carried off my heart
Leaving me behind to sink to the
    bottom of the lake of my tears?

What is love if lust of another could
    tempt me
Or, tempts the heart next to me,
Sabotaging a union so perfect?

What is love if forever is so short?
I mean, no man has peered into death
To know if love transcends
Reaching even there, too.

Is it not wise to remain alone?
Is it not smart to keep to myself?

But then...

Who's going to keep me warm in
    winter?
And when I desire to speak, will the
    walls respond?

Piérre Ramon Thomas

Who will I bother when I need
    attention?
Who's going to eat from my plate
Or drink from my cup?
There will be no eyes looking back at
    me
Except for when I look in the mirror.
And there will be no smile
    illuminating my days,
I will be left to fade to nothing in the
    darkness.

The Nomadic Poet

On Never Being Able to Keep a Man

I could always get them to come
But I could never make them stay.

Piérre Ramon Thomas

Small Town, City, Small Town (After Rupi Kaur)

(After the metaphor on pg. 97 of *Milk and Honey*)

I used to be a small town[32]—cozy, not flashy. Mom and Pop shops were the driving forces of my economy: From the market with apples and oranges in wooden crates decorating the entrance; to the hardware store with its bell indicating patrons' comings and goings; the bookstore with the cashier lost in a book on a stool by the window; to the florist with her hyacinths and roses perfuming her storefront. My town was characterized by wooden A-boards and children's laughter, monthly festivals and the smell of maple wafting from the diner. It wasn't much but it was quaint, but that wasn't enough for passersby.

For a long time, my town went abandoned; nary a handsome troubadour nor nomad stayed past a night. As the dust accumulated and the cobwebs grew, my town ached for some lonesome, wearisome traveler.

To attract visitors, I urbanized myself,[33] closing down the shops, I leveled them and bankrupted the owners. I raised up skyscrapers in their place, established fast food franchises, built an airport to the east, an expansive bus depot to the west. I knew vape shops would show I'm laxed, liquor stores would bribe newcomers; strip malls would show my desperation, and nightclubs would be booming in summer.

The Nomadic Poet

Men visited my city[34] and my city was happy, but that feeling was as fleeting as the length of their stay.

In response, I've torn down the skyscrapers, demolished both McDonalds, placed liens on the liquor stores and vape shops, and outlawed all drinking establishments.

Lawrence and Lovenia's Market has since returned. Alondra's Bookstore has reopened. The bell of Dee's Hardware is a-ringing. And Suzanne's Flowers flowers the sidewalk again.

My small town is no longer a city. All that's missing is a man in the market for a French Provincial.[35]

Piérre Ramon Thomas

Haunting Silhouettes

Shadow cast upon the wall:
An outline of me that I do not
    recognize.
I don't recognize him because
He's living a life with which I am not
    familiar.
Sometimes there are two shapes,
Two shapes of two men laughing,
    kissing, hugging.
A normal person would scream as if
    haunted by ghosts,
But I cry because my shadow is
    happier, living better than I.

I cannot take refuge in bed
Because the *non-me* silhouette follows
    me there.
No matter how much I toss and turn
    and kick,
I cannot shake the apparition lying on
    the other pillow.

The old wood creaks when I least
    expect it;
It is the sound of footsteps of a man
    who's not there.
My friends say the ghost is trying to
    terrify me—
I believe he desires to be here as much
    as I want him here

The Nomadic Poet

And this is his only way of getting my
    attention.

The second chair at the dining table
    aches for weight,
But alone I sit, eating my food;
All the while, the second silhouette
    stands beside me, hovering,
As if it is his utmost desire to sit and
    eat with me.

Escaping to my car is not an option to
    evade him,
Because sitting in the passenger seat is
    an outline of him looking at me.
And his eyes...
Although he is smiling, his eyes are
    the eyes of a mistreated dog,
Eyebrows sinking like upturned
    canoes.

IF YOU WILL INDULGE ME, I FANTASIZE ABOUT LOVE TOO MUCH

Best Love Story Ever Told

Poets to come will study us;
Authors will vie to chronicle our story.
We will be the envy of many couples
And the inspiration of a few.
I assure you, my love, they will erect
    statues of us—
Yes! In the middle of the town, we
    will be immortalized in a setting of
    bronze.
Near us, there will be a plaque which
    states:

WHAT LOVE IS AND WHAT LOVE IS SUPPOSED TO BE

Children will run around our feet;
People will come from the east and
    west to witness our glory.
Amorists will scratch their heads and
    be dumbfounded;
Psychologists will go mad because of
    us.
'Cause the world has not seen love 'til
    we came together
And Earth will weep when we pass for
    it will never see a love like ours
    again.
Our account of love will be an epic,
        the greatest,
                the best

Piérre Ramon Thomas

love story
          ever told.

In It

I am dedicated;
You, dedicated.
Our commitment towards one
    another becomes more solidified
For we are aware of the other's
    devotion to this union.
You and I,
We carve out for ourselves our own
    world in which we roam
Naked,
Unashamed,
And the words of others do not assail
    us constantly.
Consciousness has reached its zenith:
It ensures us that the cycle of love
    does not begin and end with one
But it moves back and forth between.
These eyes of ours are fixed, not on
    getting our jollies,
Temporary carnal pleasures,
But on gray hairs and cardigan
    sweaters.
We are in it
With no intentions of disavowing the
    commitment we made to one
    another—
For goodness sake, our names are
    etched into the bark of the tree.

Piérre Ramon Thomas

Aspiration

Presently, I am studying to be an astronomer
That I may know every star in the constellation of your body by name.

You Could Never Love Someone Like Me

My ever-so-tender breeze of the
 evening,
My starry, indigo sky,
My shimmering reflection of the
 moon over the lake,
May your eyes never fall on me.
For my world would turn to ash and
 eternal wisps of smoke
If you were to glance at me and turn
 away.
Look at you and then, look at me.
Your presence surpasses my humble
 status,
So I am convinced you would never
 be mine.
Although I want you, I convince
 myself that I do not
So disappointment will not befall me
 and cause me to run off into the
 distance weeping.
You are, to me, like an artifact, oh so
 statuesque in a museum,
I may look but I will never be allowed
 to touch.
Fantasy is a blessing and a curse:
For in fantasy, you are at my side—
 not even air can squeeze between
 us two;

Piérre Ramon Thomas

My curse is that I come out of my daydream and you still don't know of my existence.
Cursed man I am!

My secret desire of the innermost part of my heart,
My eyes' guilty pleasure,
My vice,
May you never know the kingdom of love I've built for you with my own two hands.
Being its only ruler, if you were to renounce your citizenship,
I might as well change my name from that which my parents gave me,
To *The-Pitiful-Man-Who-Is-A-Shell.*
If only my God would've wrought me out of the same refined gold as He did you,
Maybe, just maybe, you would notice me.
But alas, my Creator only used dust for me,
And I am a common man with nothing that makes me noteworthy.
If only I could borrow His eyes for a moment though
That I may watch you sleeping,
That way I would know you are at peace dreaming whatever dreams royal beauties dream.
Cruel life, be kind to my heart,

The Nomadic Poet

For if my love so loses a strand of hair
    due to trouble or distress,
There will be hell to pay!

My horizon early in the morning,
My infinite number of droplets of dew
    on the grass,
My medicine from St. John's-wort,
The common fabric that clothes me,
The meager shoes which encapsulate
    my feet,
The humble size of my dwelling,
Shames me into believing you would
    never affirm your devotion to me.
Let the bushes continue to hide me—
I will get my fill of you
    inconspicuously from afar.
Oh and what a fill it is!
Every day I am astounded such
    loveliness exists in human form,
That such perfection walks and talks
    and breathes among flawed
    creatures such as myself.
How can I be content with living
    knowing that whomever you will
    choose
Will not appreciate you as I know that
    I will?
What great misfortune I have!

Ah, my infant's coo,
My purpose to live,
My bear cub,

Piérre Ramon Thomas

You have cast your eyes to the left and
    spotted me.
You have parted those fine-sculpted
    lips and spoken to me.
You have even smiled.
And all the air that had escaped my
    lungs,
Which you were holding gingerly in
    your hands,
You blew back into me
(Like a kid blows a dandelion into the
    wind)
When you said, "Hello."
But when you smiled, you committed
    grand theft
Of this 24-karat, oval-cut diamond I
    keep locked up in this case.
Look at you my sweetness!
Here is me.

His Eyes

His eyes are the concierge inviting me
Into the innermost places within him.
His eyes speak a language
My body is fluent in.
His eyes make plain his pain
When his ego tries to conceal it.
His eyes are the sweetest incarceration
I desire to never break free from.
His eyes are the only hands I want
Caressing me, undressing me, tenderly
    and aggressively.
His eyes send me on expeditions
To understand the origins of him.
His eyes are the hieroglyphs I want to
    decipher,
The mysteries I desire to solve.
His eyes are the windowpanes
Upon which I do not want the rain to
    fall.
His eyes are my solar system
And naturally, I am his sun.
His eyes are the lips that cry, "Hold
    me,"
When his mouth is too ashamed to
    speak so vulnerably.
His eyes are the indicators I look to
When the stresses of life burden him
    so.
His eyes are the only wilderness
I aspire to get lost in.

Piérre Ramon Thomas

His eyes are the safehouse I escape to
When the world sets its intent on
 destroying me.
His eyes are my medicine
Whenever depression tries to engulf
 me.
His eyes contain the elements of
 dreams,
Shooing away the shadows of
 nightmares.
His eyes are the French Provincial
 home in which
I wish to spend the rest of my days.

If I Feel Safe

I am the guardian of my heart:
If I feel it is safe to let down my
    defenses,
Then, to you, I would open up.
The sword I wield to cut
And the shield I use to protect
Would become kind to you
And do you no harm.
The walls of stone which I have
    constructed,
Which almost kisses the sky,
Would become a ground for you
And carry you to my heart.
Mysteries and complexities
That dwell inside me
Would become comprehensible—
Fully explained.
I would calm and quiet the guard dogs
And they would become as puppies.
As you draw closer,
The flowers will welcome you,
Opening their petals,
And the instruments will softly
    serenade you.
You will sit in the seat of my passion
And you will be clothed with the
    sweetness of my affection.
I would look about myself,
Seeing the beauty of it all,
And I will sigh with content.

Piérre Ramon Thomas

Between Quivered Breaths

Somewhere between you touching me
And my quivered breaths,
I died a swift, sweet death
And ascended to the heaven of you.

The Consummation

The fact that we have come this far
    means I am captivated by you,
By your heart and your beauty.
For no one enters my bedroom, my
    chamber,
Unless I have been imprisoned by
    them.

Your scent surrounds me as
    atmosphere,
And I lose all myself, mesmerized.
Can this fragrance of you keep with
    me,
Never leave my nostrils?

In your embrace I become as melted
    cow butter.
I feel as high as an eagle fleeing the
    cleft of the mountaintop;
Having your hands touch my back and
    my arms and my face—
Oh, it's too much!
Can my mind take all of this delight?
Will I overflow like a vase that has had
    its fill of water?
Will I tear like a bag that has had its
    fill of articles?

Sorry I don't come to you with big,
    fancy words

Piérre Ramon Thomas

And I don't have a carrier's pouch full
    of poetic sayings;
All I have is what I know to say and
    how to say it.

The taste of your lips with mine is like
    the mixing of lavender and
    sandalwood;
You *can* have one without the other
    but together, they're a delicacy.
I cannot compare the flavor of your
    lips to anything on Earth
For it would be falsehood.
Indeed, your flavor is that of your
    own, unique to yourself.

Let me remove your clothes and
    expose that bare body
I have been longing to see since the
    rising of the sun.
Let my hands explore every region of
    your body
But restrain not my lips, lest they
    become jealous.
I tell you, not one iota of your body is
    abhorred by me,
Turn me loose if, to you, it seems that
    way.
Every flaw you think you have, pulls
    me even more into you.

Alright, enough lips!

Let me restrict myself unless I
    overindulge and become used to
    you;
I have taken just enough to satisfy me
    until our next encounter.

Hold on to me while we are
    intertwined.
I want to know—*I want to feel* you are
    as close as possible to me.
When our bodies touch, I want to
    forsake the garments that
    constrain us, once and for all.

Can this moment last forever?
Does there have to be an end?

Piérre Ramon Thomas

The Army I Formed for You

The army of glittering lights flaunt their glory in the indigo sky.

The division of dolphins trill excitedly and arc above the waters.

The corps of honeybees produce their sweet nectar in busy buzzy hives.

The brigade of birds chorally sing their morning melodies in the trees.

The battalion of butterflies flutter their colored wings amidst green gardens.

The company of seamstresses skillfully weave silks, satins, and linens in their shops.

The platoon of Earth's waters ebb and flow, shimmer and foam about the coasts.

The squad of celestial bodies perform their daily, axial twirls around the sun.

The team of continents yield their fruit and abundance from the earth.

And I, your patriotic soldier, stand eagerly at attention,

The Nomadic Poet

My decorated four-star general.

I anxiously await whatever word you may speak

To fulfill whatsoever your lovely heart may request

Or, if it is for love—*love*.

Piérre Ramon Thomas

My Only Desire

I have wanted for nothing more
Than for my arms to be your fortified
    haven
Those moments when your strength
    escapes you
And you need a solitary moment to
    feel safe until your strength
    returns.

I have yearned for nothing more
Than for my eyes to be the things that
    flatter you
If ever you need to feel handsome—
*and men do need to be validated from
time to time*—
My eyes will tell you all you need to
    hear.

I have ached for nothing more
Than for my hands to be surveyors
    exploring the territory of your
    body,
For every plot of land on your body to
    be warmed by the sun[10]
Causing your deep earth[12] to delight
    with giddiness.

I have craved for nothing more
Than for my heart to wash over you
Enclosing you,

The Nomadic Poet

Enveloping you,
Folding over you,
And expanding upon you.

Piérre Ramon Thomas

Mementos

I opened all the cabinets in our house,
Showed him all the ceramic flasks I
    stored,
Even brought some out of hiding and
    placed them in the open.
"These, my love, hold all the tears I've
    ever cried,
Tears I've cried whenever I mourned
    the absence of a lover."
He asked me why I still kept them,
    seeing that he is here now.
I replied, "I keep them as a reminder
    of my life before you.
I save them to remind me of the
    bitterness by which I was
    possessed.
In case my fallible mind fails me and I
    forget to be kind to your heart,
Just in case I abandon my
    commitment to envelop you in my
    tenderness,
I will pick up these vials and think
    back to what it was like,
When the darkness of sorrow washed
    over me."

After he heard my reasoning,
He himself added to my collection.

The Moment

I knew he was perfect for me when
I saw every word, every line, and every
    stanza I ever wrote
Inscribed into his skin.
I traced my fingers over the words:
He was unaware of what I saw.

Piérre Ramon Thomas

willful exposition

usually i am a man of capitalizations
    and punctuation marks
without them i consider my poems
    naked
but just for the sheer pleasure of
    baring myself to you
i am forsaking the practice of clothing
    my poetry
in hopes that you would witness the
    nudity of my words
and equate it to my vulnerability to
    you
if you notice my love look i am not
    using periods
for there are no barriers no stops no
    endpoints
nothing within me that is cut off from
    you
i have given up *temporarily may i admit*
    commas
for i do not want my love to pause or
    be held back from you at all
let it be a neverending flow
and although your passion often
    inspires exclamation points
i have omitted them in order for my
    praise of you to speak on its own
    behalf
you crystal bowl of ambrosia
you glass carafe of mango nectar

without periods
there is an expectation of more
even at the end of these words
i refuse to close with a period
for i want to convey to your
    understanding
that my love has no end
it continues to be
this composition may come to an end
but *know* that my love does not

...

Piérre Ramon Thomas

When Forever Is Interrupted

While planning
The course of our future,
Thoughts of death
Choked my mind.

In prayer,
I asked Spirit
That if I die first,
That my spirit
Would surround you
Like the air you breathe
Until you joined me.

I cannot bear to think
What my world
Would be like
If you were to die first.
But if you do,
If my God so allows,
If He has any reserves of grace,
Any,
Any left to spare at all,
May your lovely spirit
Keep with me
And feed me strength,
The strength that I
Will undoubtedly need,
To continue living,
Day to day,
Without you.

My Government

Draft your constitution.
I assure you, from this day forward,
I will uphold every line to the letter.
Declare to me, your patriot, the Five
    Tenets upon which this union is
    established,
That I may run to show my eagerness
    and loyalty.

"Through the sincerity of love, we will build.
On trust, we will strengthen.
By compromise and sacrifice, we will grow.
In the zeal of fidelity, we will sustain.
And by renewing ourselves from time to time
    with the fire of rekindling,
Our love will extend beyond time."

As you have said, my love,
So will it be obeyed.
I pledge my allegiance to you—
Ah! If only you knew how giddy I am
    to please you!
This is a type of monocracy that keeps
    the land at peace;
For by you, I am tamed,
Without you, I am a wild, rabid animal
    that struggles with self-control.
Wrap me inside of your flag.
Make me a garland of the flowers of
    your country and crown me.

Piérre Ramon Thomas

Say that I am your one and only
    citizen—
Promise there will not be another.
My love, you are my government;
I am governed by you.

On Account of You

(Inspired by "Love All Over Me" by Monica)

You.
You were the key
To unlocking metaphors,
Similes within me.
It was you
Who found the lever
That triggered the switch
That opened the passageway
To the library
Of the volumes of poetry stored
In the secret places
In my heart.
It was your love
That taught me
What real love is
That I, in turn,
Would be able to
Articulate to others,
In rhyme or free verse
What this beautiful abstract is.

It was your soul
That I,
Before we even knew
Of each other's existence,
Wrote romantic prophecies of.
Some days,
I jokingly say
I wrote and spoke

Piérre Ramon Thomas

You into existence.
That the reverberation
Of what I
Would one day write
Reached back
Through time
To reach God's ears
And upon Him hearing
Words that I
Would one day speak,
Took those words
And fashioned them
Into you.

You were the reason
For which
God told me:
"You must be
The best version
Of yourself
You can be."
For you,
I was put in fire
Time after time
To become
The refined man
Who stands before you
Today.
Pure gold!

You brought color
To a world
Of black and white.
You brought

The Nomadic Poet

A wave of heat
And ushered me
Out of the Ice Age,
A world once
Frozen over.
I don't know
How you did it,
But the lakes of my tears
Have all dried up
Since you arrived.
Slowly,
I am beginning
To forget
What sorrow is.
All of this
On account
Of you.

Piérre Ramon Thomas

Is Time Still Time Concerning Us?

Explain how time shared with you
 feels like decades,
But when we have to separate for a
 while,
It feels like we were cheated,
That we didn't have enough time
 together.
Is time still time when we're together?
Can it still be termed such?

When we are enjoying one another,
Time[25] releases us from its limitations.
It looks down upon us and delights to
 see our lovemaking,
So it steps aside.
It only returns when we come back
 down to Earth,
When Reality[26] says, "The two of you
 cannot stay together this way all
 the time."
Then we say to Time, "You deceived
 us! We needed more time."
Time replies, "Do you think you are
 the first pair of lovebirds
To be displeased with me?
I am obligated to a higher order:
I orchestrate the sun and moon;
I make the day and the night arrive
 when it is supposed;
I oversee the four seasons;

Winter, spring, summer and autumn
    must arrive according to schedule.
The passing of the weeks, months and
    years cannot stop for the sake of
    you two.
But I do give you a gift in the midst of
    all my work:
I remove from your senses the regard
    of time for you to enjoy your
    sessions of intimacy."

Piérre Ramon Thomas

Fluent

Hearing the words I wrote,
The same words I conceived and gave
    birth to,
Tumble and dive from the same lips I
    exploit and kiss,
Set me on perpetual fire that no water
    could dare extinguish.

Later, when my lips were caressing his
    lips,
I noticed a spiciness that wasn't quite
    there before;
The all-consuming fire that is me finds
    the spiciness of his lips sweet
Because the words that constitute my
    world is now the language he
    speaks.

Our Lovemaking

Many o' nights we found ourselves
    coasting over the smooth sounds
    of Sade Adu,
Her velvety voice escorting us through
    emotions and sensations in search
    of ecstasy.
Having no choreographer, our bodies
    invented dance routines
Of rhythmic thrusts and synchronized
    strokes in pursuit of bliss.
We borrowed the hands of men like
    Duke Ellington and Little Richard,
Like the prodigies, we played the
    piano keys on each other's bodies
    with intuitive precision.
It was never our intent to disturb the
    neighbors,
Yet we were equally reluctant to mute
    the sound effects of our passion;
If wolves cannot be muzzled,
Neither could we.
Our mouths became experts in the
    regions that induced temporary
    insanity,
However, we only visited those
    locations for a short time
Because we always returned to our
    hometowns
Which are each other's lips.

Piérre Ramon Thomas

You take great pride in your success
    of the colonization of my body.
I remember when you were just a
    mere frontiersman exploring its
    undiscovered territories.
Today, there is not one tract of land
    on my body
That does not wave the flag of your
    country[36] boldly and proudly.
You have made a habit of skiing down
    the slopes of my back,
For your expertise, I stole the gold
    medal from Olympian Tommy
    Moe and awarded you with the
    honor.
With the pencil of your fingers, you
    have traced and retraced the
    outlines of me
So much so that your knowledge of
    my body cancels my own.
How did you know handling me like a
    shotgun
Was one of the many secrets to
    pleasuring me?
How did you know that bracing my
    fore-end with one hand
And gripping my stock with the other
Not only is proper weapon
    management
But are the fundamentals to firing my
    trigger?

I am no stranger to hiking up and
    down your pleasure trail;

The Nomadic Poet

It is the only exercise that I do
    without protest.
Onward from there, I spent many o'
    days surveying the grassy valleys
    of your chest,
Just so I can scale the mountains of
    your back.
I used to tell myself I would never
    climb mountains because it was
    far too dangerous,
But having been acquainted with your
    mountain, I disregard the risk.
And if I fall, so be it,
As long as our bed remains my
    landing pad,
You become the mountain lion and I
    become the deer.
I have often envied the talents of
    sculptors
Those moments you stood naked,
Unembarrassed
Of every square footage of your bare
    skin inviting in the light;
I wanted to grab the nearest block of
    marble,
Chisel a representation of your
    physique,
Put it on display in our home,
Then donate it to the Smithsonian
    upon our deaths.

Who says the male form is not artistic?

Piérre Ramon Thomas

Now, I am no volcanologist by no
    stretch of the imagination,
But the eruption of our volcanoes
    puts Mount Vesuvius to shame.

Escape to Utopia

We secured each other's hands in our own hands and ran,
Left all behind and escaped this present world.
The gavel of their law no longer beats down upon us;
Successfully, we have evaded the prison of their thoughts and the artillery of their judgment.
In this utopia, only the law of love rules us
And we answer to no one but the King.

Piérre Ramon Thomas

What I Answer When He Calls

When he calls out, "Indigo."[37]
I answer, "Yes, Cerulean?"[38]

When he purrs, "My heaven."
I respond, "My paradise."

When he growls, "Koala Bear."
I smile, "Yes, Grizzly?"

When he sings, "Lavender."
My heart swoons, "Sandalwood."

When we joke, he teases, "Key Lime Pie."
I play along, ribbing, "Mr. Gummi Bears."

When he takes me by the hand, he says, "Ocean."
Gleefully, I beam, "Mountain."

When we defend ourselves, he asks, "You got my 6?"
To which I yell back, "Affirmative!"

When he pulls me into him, he inhales, "My home."
Exhaling, I assure him, "Always."

When he starts with, "Oh, moo-oon..."
I anticipate his words with, "Yes, my sun?"

The Swordsmen: The Warrior and the Poet

(A Poetic Tale)

We never flaunted ourselves, strutting
>   around, looking for trouble,
But bothersome wolves frequently
>   attempted to make hares out of
>   us.
Whenever legions of men besieged us,
We became knife-stabbing, dagger-
>   throwing, Falchion-wielding
>   swordsmen.

Before our initial encounter, he told
>   me how he often visited the
>   tavern
Where I recited my compositions to
>   rooms full of poetry
>   connoisseurs and drunkards.
What intrigued him about me was that
>   my verses were soft and tender,
Beating down and eroding the rough,
>   coarse places within him.
He noted how I, like him, carried a
>   sword in a sheath at my hip,
But wondered why my form didn't
>   show the signs of battle like his.

After I was devoured by the voracity
>   in his eyes,

Piérre Ramon Thomas

His unapologetic masculinity
    entangled me in the web of his
    appeal.
Unlike most men, he flamboyantly,
    unashamedly sported his
    mustache and full beard,
Hair even dared to grow on his arms
    and strived to grow beyond the
    top button of his shirt.
Overtaken by his Barbarian-like
    charm,
I drunkenly succumbed to his
    masculine devices.

Behind closed doors, he shared with
    me that he was a valiant warrior,
    a killer of men,
He confided that, much to his
    displeasure, he watched life
    drain from many men's eyes.
He explained that he killed only when
    absolutely necessary
And that he never raised his sword
    without provocation.
Caressing his beautiful face, I assured
    him,
From that moment on, he will never
    have to fight alone ever again.

As certain as the Great Spirit,
Men, uncomfortable with our love,
    made enemies out of us.
War was constantly waged against us,
    both verbally and physically.

The Nomadic Poet

In defense of our safety, we had a
 tradition of making our swords
 touch, standing back-to-back,
And charging forward, expertly
 swinging our blades against all
 the monsters and beasts that
 surrounded us.

Piérre Ramon Thomas

A Profession

My love, your love to me is so
    extraordinary,
I am constantly compelled to celebrate
    the greatness of your love with
    our family and friends;
The soirees I organize are nothing but
    occasions masked to applaud you,
Your love deserves recognition,
    revelry, standing ovations.
So attentive, so anticipatory your love
    is,
I do not have time to need or want for
    anything before you've already
    acted.
The way you attempt to understand
    the essence of me, from my
    genesis to my terminus,
Not even the greatest novel ever
    penned knows the sweet delight I
    know.
To my shame, I admit I am spoiled:
On account of your tender-loving care
    I have no need for the love of
    others.
Who is she or he that has taught you
    how to love so thoroughly,
Let me kiss the hand of the teacher
    who has bestowed such an
    education upon you?

The Nomadic Poet

May their soul, whoever they may be,
  be forever blessed.
Let their days overflow with the same
  love that you render to me.
He who does not have the parameters
  of his heart filled with an all-
  encompassing love
Is a poor man, despite how many
  earthly possessions he possesses;
In the era before you were known to
  me, I lived in squalor,
As I look around myself today, I am
  the wealthiest man, enriched with
  your tender care.
I have no need nor do I want for
  anyone else;
You are enough, more than enough;
Superfluous is what your parents
  should've named you.
Every time I meditate on your love,
I am overcome with gratefulness.
I beam with excitement knowing out
  of all the millions
  circumnavigating this Earth,
You fixed your gaze upon me and
  chose me to pour your love into.
There must be some sort of medal
  with which I can award you
For braving this world with me, hand-
  in-hand, unapologetically;
There must exist a Meritorious Love
  Medal I can drape around your
  neck

Piérre Ramon Thomas

For valiantly, courageously displaying
your love to me regardless of who
sees.
How is it I have missed you before I
met you?
Usually a person can only miss that
which they know;
I assure you, many times, *many, many,
many* times,
I mourned the lack of a mature, deep,
resounding love.
There is jubilation everywhere I go
now;
My humble spirit sports a warm smile
and disseminates cheerfulness to
all passersby.
Such an amazing feat that the universe
can contain
The weight and the volume of the
love I carry for you inside me;
One would think the universe would
fold in on itself on account of me,
Yet it guarantees me that it exists to
contain an immense amount of a
substance.
Thank you for taking this journey with
me fellow traveler;
I appreciate you've chosen me to
accompany you on life's
adventures.
O how I wish there was no inevitable
end to our journey,
But rest assured, sweet soul, whether
in flesh or in spirit, I will be with

you, from your last seconds and
beyond.

Piérre Ramon Thomas

Persuading Mr. Self-Sufficient

He used his powers of persuasion
To convince me, Mr. Self-Sufficient
    himself,
Not only that I needed him,
But that not having him would be the
    greatest loss I would ever
    experience.

Gray Hairs

(A Poetic Tale)

He saw me isolating and examining
    my grays in the mirror.
He noticed the trepidation in my face
    confronting the decay of my body.
He neglected to tell me that I
    offended him the other day,
When I asked him if he would ever
    leave me for a younger, baby-
    faced man.

He thought to himself:
How can I leave you when my
    history—our history—
Is written in the grays of your hair?
Every argument, every "you're
    sleeping on the couch tonight
    buddy!"
Is transcribed there.
Our journeys to the corners of the
    Earth
Are recorded in the passport of your
    strands.
The casualties of conflicts we
    triumphed over
Are all buried in the battleground of
    your curls.
All the times we made love and came
    close to spontaneous combustion

Piérre Ramon Thomas

Are journaled in the diary of your
    tresses.

His thoughts continued:
How can I abandon you Beautiful,
When the hieroglyphs of my kisses are
    written on the walls of your skin?
How can I leave you when I know
    with certainty
Another will not love me as I *know*
    you have?

Poetry didn't slide as easily off his
    tongue.
Mustering up all the words he could
    manage,
He responded:
"All I can say is that I give you my
    word I will never leave you,
But only Time[25] could testify to that
    truth."

In the Beginning

I envied the sun, I envied the moon,
For they were permanent fixtures in
    your world.
So I tasked myself with the mission of
    winning your heart
That I too would become a celestial
    body in your sky.

Your eyes lassoed me
And I didn't struggle or fight;
I gave in to your abduction
And said, "Have your way with me."

The marriage of our minds took place
Long before the meeting of our
    bodies;
Two mental corporations merged
Becoming the parent company to
    many thriving spiritual,
    philosophical, and poetic
    subsidiaries.

Your hands had this sort of
    supernatural power
That made one's knees become wind-
    blown mummies;
Your arms had this divine ability
To exorcise the demons of insecurity
    and depression.

Piérre Ramon Thomas

Passion for you was so compressed within me,
I wanted this walking English lexicon to explode
And have the shrapnel of all the beautiful words in existence
Come together to become a book of odes and sonnets dedicated to you.

I Present My Heart to You

Upon a velvet, royal blue pillow,
Adorned with gold fringe on all four
   sides,
Sits ever so humbly nothing but
Fragility, vulnerability, and fervent
   passion.

I beg you, please, O handsome,
   rugged one,
Please do not make a sport out of my
   heart;
Do not find it amusing or recreational
To kick and headbutt my heart
   around.

Not only do I reveal to you my
   beauty, the very best of me,
I also confess to you my ugliness;
Every flaw, every weakness, every
   insecurity, all of my troubled
   history,
I lay bare before you—even if it is to
   my embarrassment and to my
   shame.

See the fire my heart produces?
Take it and light multiple lamps.
Place the lamps in every room of your
   house

Piérre Ramon Thomas

So the fire that emanates from my
    heart can be the heat that keeps
    you warm and cozy.

The fact that you can see this
    multicolored, yet visually
    invisible,[39] fire
Is a testament to the honesty of your
    care for me;
The fact that you can take your finger
    and caress this blaze
Speaks to the purity of your
    tenderness.

I present my heart to you
And the steel, dual-swing gates, once
    chained and locked,
Are now opened wide
And many glorious wonders await you
    inside.

Nursed to Health

Before you came, I was
　　malnourished—
No, not from food,
But from love.
My bones were visible through my
　　thin skin,
My stomach ached not knowing when
　　my next filling would come.
I saw others, with light in their faces,
Fat from their indulgences.
Although I did not want to beg,
I, too, became a beggar.
My body was as frail as the holy men
　　who fast.
My eyes were glazed from excessive
　　tears.
I fed myself with morsels which were
　　thrown from their lofty places,
I forsook any remaining pride.

But our first encounter gave me life,
My heart was assured of your interest.
Your voice to my ears was as a song
　　of love,
I was hypnotized.
You could've requested anything from
　　me,
Being your puppet, I would've
　　obeyed.
Your kisses fattened me,

Piérre Ramon Thomas

And my skin grew full.
Your embrace was meat for my soul,
I was reluctant to be anywhere else.
Your touch sent oxygen into my
    lungs,
The air became sweet again.
Our cuddling together bandaged my
    wounds,
Making me understand I wasn't
    unlovable.
Your comprehension of me nursed
    me to complete health,
Seeing my unfolded mind in all its
    rawness.

Allegiance

Within these iron walls, you are safe;
I dare a miscreant to poke out his
    chest and threaten such beautiful
    flesh.
Twenty-four/seven I stand watch,
Patrolling from tower to tower along
    the walls of the stronghold
Ensuring your security, Your Majesty.
What I do is not an obligatory
    occupation that renders no
    reward—
Nay! It is a labor of love, for which, I
    have joyfully volunteered.
All the citizens throughout the
    kingdom know to whom my
    loyalty belongs
And it is public knowledge for whom
    I will go to war.

Piérre Ramon Thomas

The Creation of You: A Revelation

When my Creator was forming you,
He pointed to the nearest boulder and
    bellowed, "Come out!"
He made sure that the lines of your
    design were well-defined.
He made sure the earth of your body
    was tender-firm.
When He made you,
He gave you the muscled neck and
    jawbone of a stallion,
He duplicated profound lines and
    curves found in urban
    architecture.
For your midsection, He gave you the
    torso of the Silverback,
For your hirsuteness, He suited you
    with the pelt of the American
    bison.
The wingspan of your back He
    stretched
That it can be measured perfectly in
    horizontal skyscrapers,
He broadened your shoulders
Until they occupied the distance
    between America and Europe.
He patted His hands on the
    floorgrounds of the woods,
The morning after the evening rains,
Patted you from crown to sole

The Nomadic Poet

And fragranced your skin with its
    smell.
He opened the cupboards of your
    arms,
Filled the shelves with the strength
    and power of charging
    rhinoceroses.

As mythical as you may seem,
My account is by no means an
    exaggeration of your creation.

Piérre Ramon Thomas

The Marionettist

Your hands on my lower back
Is equivalent to a puppeteer holding
    the strings over his marionette.
Just be careful how you wield your
    power,
With your hands resting there, I am
    but a weak man.

Three Men, Three Diamond Vessels

(A Poetic Tale)

Three men carried one diamond vessel
 of their own.
Their vessels were hollow,
Shaped like thick icicles.
Enclosed in their vessels
Were their hearts—the essence of
 them.
The sight of their hearts were glowing
 lights
And the capsules were glass-like so
 each man was cautious carrying it.

The first man gave his heart to his
 lover
And said, "Be mindful of how you
 care for my heart:
I am entrusting it to you.
Just as I will safeguard your heart,
Be attentive to mine."
In the beginning, she obeyed his
 advice;
Protected it as if it was the wealthiest
 possession in the world.
Then,
She committed infidelity against him.
His vessel cracked and his light grew a
 little dim.
The man forgave her
Since he knew temptation was strong.

Piérre Ramon Thomas

Then,
She vexed his spirit with judgmental
    words
And heaped upon him unnecessary
    abuse.
The man's vessel cracked much more
    and his light grew even dimmer.
Then,
There came a point where she didn't
    love him anymore;
Her feelings for the man faded and
    died.
The man's light went completely out
    and his vessel ruptured.

The second man waited for a lover to
    give his vessel to;
He smiled when he observed other
    couples in love.
In the beginning, his light was so
    bright,
It sometimes blinded him.
Over time, still with no one to give his
    vessel to,
His light slowly grew dim
        And dimmer.
It was only when he had lost hope in
    love—
At least for himself—
Was when his light went completely
    out
And his vessel shattered in his
    presence.

The Nomadic Poet

The third man gave his vessel to his
    lover.
She was mature;
Intelligent in the art of love
    And how to express it.
She kissed the heart,
Caressed the heart,
Embraced the heart,
Conversed with the heart,
And attended to the heart.
Over time, the light of the man's heart
    grew brighter and brighter.
Needless to say, the glass-like vessel
    fortified.

The man comforted his two
    companions for their sufferings
Since he knew love is a rare
    commodity.

Piérre Ramon Thomas

From Web & Loom

At the beginning of time,
You and I, our hearts and souls,
Two thin, hair-like strands,
Were twisted together into one thread
And woven into the fabric of forever.

Even when the Weaver[40]
Cuts the tapestry,[41]
You and I, our thread,
Will squeeze tighter together
Hoping wherever our thread lands or
    goes,
We will always be together.

Sometimes the Prey Is the Predator

I am as coy as a cloud-draped moon
When I want him to devour me;
And I become as bold as an
 unimpeded sun in the cloudless,
 cerulean sky
When *I* crave *him*.

Piérre Ramon Thomas

Street Preacher

If your love for me doesn't inspire you
To go door-to-door,
Bringing the good news to your
    neighbors,
Both far and wide,
Of how you feel about me—

If your love for me doesn't motivate
    you
To stand on street corners and
    medians on the roads,
Proclaiming to all passersby
Willing to listen
About the man whom you adore—

If your love for me doesn't compel
    you
To go about preaching the gospel
    according to...*you*,
Sharing scriptures from your
    Romantic Bible
Of your musings of me,
Converting all nonbelievers into
    pastors, prophets and evangelists
    of love—

Then...

A Perfect Argument

(A Poetic Tale)

We screamed so loud the neighbors were frightened.
We over-talked one another, strong voices drowning out relevant points.
We kept interrupting each other, unwilling to yield our positions.
I threw a vase at the wall,
Water, glass, and flowers left their marks;
You kicked the hamper,
Deploying soiled clothes here and there.

Fed up with the stubbornness of one other,
We both retreated to separate rooms.

After some time had passed,
I, as you've also done in times past,
Approached you humbly.
You witnessed how my heart was cupped in my hands.
I apologized;
My nation[42] signed a treaty with your nation.

Police banged on our door,

Piérre Ramon Thomas

We answered with arms secured
    around one another.
They entered and noted the chaotic
    state of our house
And said, "We received complaints
    from the neighbors of a
    disturbance."
Looking at each other, we smiled,
Replying, "Apologies officers, we had
    an argument earlier,
But now we're at peace."

Noticing no bruises, seeing no cause
    for arrest,
The officers exited with a warning,
    "Next time, just try to keep it
    down."

We reconciled several more times that
    night,
Forgetting whatever petty thing we
    were arguing about to begin with.
We waited until the next day to clean
    up the mess;
Holding each other throughout the
    night,
We both laughed at our foolishness.

I Saw You Before I Met You

Before you made your grand entrance,
Gaiting with the ease of a twilight's
    breeze,
I dreamt lucid dreams of you.
Details of your face were hidden
But schematics of your heart and
    mind were fully laid out before me
Like an unfolded blueprint.

That explains why from time to time,
I playfully pinch your arm.
It is to assure me that you are really
    here
And not *still* a figment of my
    imagination.

Piérre Ramon Thomas

Beau of the Ball

(A Poetic Tale)

I spotted my love telling humorous
    anecdotes,
Enthralling the guests sitting at our
    table.
He had that sort of magnetic
    personality
That attracted people to him.
I, on the other hand, could never be
    as charismatic,
Yet there was something about me
    that arrested him.
I sat in the empty seat beside him,
Patiently waited to find an opening to
    speak.
When successful, I leaned over and
    whispered in his ear,
"Would you like to dance with me?"

Once he brought his storytelling to an
    end,
I took him by the hand and led him to
    the dance floor.
Neither of us were classically trained;
We were just two amateurs
    unbothered by vicious scrutiny.
Our hands interlocked like puzzle
    pieces;
We settled the other hand on each
    other's backs

And slow-danced to Vandross' "If
   This World Were Mine".[43]
Who knew gods could dance?
My love, to me, was Alvin Ailey
   reincarnated.
He smelled like an ocean breeze,
He was tender as a mother
   breastfeeding her newborn.
I felt sorry for other men:
No face could equate to the
   supremacy of his face.

Watching me stare at him, he smiled
   that addictive half-smile
He makes when he gets nervous.
Shyly, he asked as he looked away,
   "What?"
Beaming the light of my smile upon
   him, I echoed, "What?"
"You got that look in your eyes you
   get when you're thinking deep
   thoughts about me."
It was my turn to be shy,
I looked away, still beaming.

"You know?
Totaling up the sum of you,
Everything and all that makes you *you*,
My appraisal has determined that you
   are invaluable;
There is no other man who could
   replace who you are and what you
   do for me."
Caressing his cheek, I continued,

Piérre Ramon Thomas

"How blessed am I that I get to touch
 the same man
My God in heaven fashioned with His
 own two hands!"

At the end of my words,
He took me and kissed me as if the
 apocalypse was happening at that
 very moment.

More Than a Sexual Creature

Tell me all of your thoughts and
    feelings
And in return I will do the same.
Give me all of affection and
    tenderness
And in return I will do the same.
Give me all of your conversation
And in return I will do the same.
I am more than a sexual creature;
My needs extend beyond my desire
For your body pressed against mine.
I have more to offer you besides my
    physique,
Size,
Or stamina.
I know how to keep your attention
Without our bodies touching one
    another.

Piérre Ramon Thomas

Well Never Empty

Whenever you come to this well—
    Daily if it is your pleasure—
The spring of love will always be fresh
    for you,
My companion.
You will never have to wonder
If I find you breathtaking,
For my hands will let you know,
My eyes will not be silent,
My heart will envelop you,
And your mind will be at ease.

Perfection Personified

There are none that could compare to
    your unblemished visage,
Encountering you in this desert,[44]
    initially, I mistook you for a
    mirage.
Yet here you stand, my liege, made of
    blood and flesh and bone,
Vowing your eternal loyalty, your
    heart is mine, mine alone.

Our love is pure and sacred, no text
    could ever vilify,
For we have discovered a world
    unencumbered, beyond cerulean
    sky.

Exhibitions of your power cause me
    to forfeit self-control,
Losing my wits I become magnetized,
    I collapse within your hold.

Make your home upon my chest,
    drink me as if you die of thirst,
Whisper lyrics of your musings of me,
    with statements unrehearsed.
Tell me your fears, my warrior, that
    my arms may fulfill their
    occupation,

Piérre Ramon Thomas

Cry—without judgment—if you need;
know you have refuge in this
nation.

Fix your intent on settling, there is no
more need to roam,
The height of the battle is over, within
me you've found a home.
You suspect your imperfections will
cause my interest to fade,
However, I am blind to your flaws,
you were expertly made.

That Time When We Made Love for Forever

Do you remember the time when we
    made love for forever,
When the Earth stopped spinning,
    time paused,
When the stars in space were our
    backdrop,
And our moans were heard in other
    galaxies?

Do you remember the time when our
    bodies resembled twisted rope,
When there were no such things as
    YOU or I, only WE

    WE WERE, WE ARE &
    WE WILL BE

When we were imprinted into the
    Book of Time,[45] making us
    immortal?

Do you remember the time when our
    souls communed with one another
— *Absent of words* —
When my heart spoke directly to your
    heart,
Vowing never to harm you, promising
    never to leave you,
Proclaiming my devotion, loudly and
    boldly renouncing all others?

Piérre Ramon Thomas

Do you remember the time when you were a harpist,
When you, by your knowledge as a world-renowned musician,
Knew when to play the strings vigorously and when to play them softly
Leaving the harp behind panting in ecstasy?

I will never forget.

Spiders & Centipedes

His mouth signed a verbal contract
Promising he'll always be my
    designated spider- and centipede-
    killer.
I watched my superhero, whose
    costume hung in our closet,
Use his bug-killing superpowers to
    defeat the centipede villain
Who had been terrorizing my life
    from the 30 seconds he scurried
    into my line of view.

Later that night, any doubts of my
    love was reaffirmed
All unsettling thoughts clouding his
    mind,
Dissipated
Bringing him sweet assurance and a
    peaceful slumber.

Piérre Ramon Thomas

The Morning After

(A Poetic Tale)

The side where he was sleeping was
    ice cold;
One would think nary a body had
    never occupied that space.
His clothes, which I had removed
And tossed across the room in
    inconvenient irritation,
Had disappeared from their places;
The floor, the desk, and the chaise
    were bare.
The silence that greeted me I rejected;
I, at least, hoped I would awaken to
    the sounds of a snoring giant—
Which would've been sweet music to
    my ears.

Yet, as I sniffed the air, I could not
    fail to smell Sri Lankan cinnamon
    and chocolate,
Two smells I could never conceive
    marrying one another in fragrant
    matrimony.
'Could I have left a candle on?' I thought,
    rushing from room to room.
It was in my nature to be
    absentminded and leave candles
    burning overnight.

The Nomadic Poet

And in my kitchen, standing as high as
    a California redwood,
There he stood putting his and my
    plates on the kitchen table.
"Good morning, Sleeping Beauty!" He
    called out, smiling the smile that
    endeared me to him.
"I made cinnamon chocolate waffles,
    scrambled eggs, and beef bacon."
"Good...morning?" I responded, still a
    little disoriented and surprised.
I enjoyed the view of him in my too-
    small shirt, which, on him, was a
    midriff, and my undergarments.
"I mixed my clothes in with yours and
    put them in the washer;
I had to steal some of your clothes; I
    didn't know if you had a rule
    against nakedness."
Beaming, I replied, "No, it's fine.
    Nakedness is fine, too."
I could not help but to conduct an
    out-of-body overview of the scene
    I was enacting.
He turned to the stove to retrieve the
    warmed honey, calling back,
"Remind me to get some slippers as
    well. I had to steal those too—"
I had run up behind him and wrapped
    my arms around him as tightly as I
    could.
I rested my cheek on his back before I
    kissed his spine.

Piérre Ramon Thomas

"What's wrong?" His voice fluctuated.
    "What is it?"
Hearing nothing for a while, he
    stroked my forearms to comfort
    me.
I inhaled his scent through my shirt
    and marveled at the artwork of his
    scalp and neck before sighing,
"You're still here. You didn't leave."

He turned around and said, as he had
    many times before,
"I've told you: yes, I wanted you—
    God yes, I wanted you!—but I also
    want *you*."

Poor, but Rich

We don't have gold trimmings, marble
    floors or a backyard pool,
But we have a place to lay our heads.
We can't afford Louie Vuitton, Gucci
    or Christian Louboutin,
But we have items with which to
    clothe our naked bodies.
Our refrigerator is never filled with
    lobster, filet mignon or Veuve
    Clicquot,
But we always have just enough to last
    us through the week.
We don't have money to travel,
But our arguments are few and very
    short-lived.
Our bank account has never seen the
    number 5,000,
But there is an abundance of laughter
    in our walls.
We may not be able to go to fancy
    restaurants,
But trust and fidelity are staples in our
    home.

Our ceiling leaks constantly.
Our wages are never enough.
We live paycheck-to-paycheck.
We depend on government assistance.
Things are always breaking down.
Many bills, every month, go unpaid.

Piérre Ramon Thomas

We name and make friends with the
  neighborhood rats.
The homeless, at times, seem
  wealthier than us.

But, at least, we genuinely like and
  care for each other.
We crave each other's presence.
Our smiles continue toward one
  another.
Our cheap mattress has plenty of
  dents from our lovemaking.
And most importantly, we retain our
  faith in the Supreme One.

Extremely poor we may be,
Yes. But,
Overwhelmingly rich we are...

...In love.

Garlic Spaghetti

(A Poetic Tale)

My love snuck up from behind
While I was in the kitchen cooking my
    famous garlic spaghetti.
He had a tradition of wrapping his
    arms around me tightly
And kissing me on my neck.
    Erykah Badu had taught him well.[46]
He made it clear that he only came
To collect his payment of kisses.
Wanting to oblige him, I warned,
"I have been tasting the sauce along
    the way
And my breath is pungent from the
    garlic."
He turned me around, saying,
"Although I am addicted to the flavor
    of your lips all on their own,
It is still a treat to taste them enhanced
    with the flavor of herbs and
    spices.
Besides, I do not kiss you solely for
    the taste alone,
I kiss you because I need your lips for
    the sake of my sanity."

With delight, he sampled the tomato
    sauce.
With pleasure, he tasted the garlic.

Piérre Ramon Thomas

Past Self < Present Self

I'm glad you didn't know me back
    then,
Back when I was foolish, immature,
    and toxic.

But if ever you learn of the foolish,
    ignorant man I was,
I hope you stay on account of the man
    I am today.*

> *The version of the man you see today is the result of many years of growth, self-improvement, and evolution.*

All to Show You My Love

Before I sent the wind to dance
    around you,
I ordered it to caress your cheek;
It carried my profession of love in a
    breeze,
Whispered it to you soft-spoken.

Once I commanded the rain clouds to
    swarm,
Droplets began diving exponentially;
I spoke to the rain to spare you,
It respected the shelter of love.

I held out my palm, caught lightning
    in my fist,
Released it back from where it came;
I raised my other hand to signal
    thunder,
The sound mimicked the intensity of
    my love.

I waved my hands above me,
Directed rain clouds to go away;
The clean sky flaunted the sun,
I invited white clouds to return.

Piérre Ramon Thomas

Love Me in All Elements

If your passion is fire,
Let the flames sear me
From skin to soul.
If your heart
Is a body of water,
I hope I drown
To its lowermost depth.
If your arms are earth,
May they bury me
'Til I am deep beneath the surface.
If the fervency and zeal of your attraction
To me is air,
I pray I am swept away
And never find my footing again.

At a Loss for Words

How can I call myself a wordsmith,
If I fail to constantly find the words,
Words with which to describe the
    whole of you,
When moments call for it?

I fear, not even the most scholarly of
    linguists
Knows of such a word—or words—
To attribute to the glory of you
Whenever my heart swells with joy
    speaking of you.
I deduce that even in their scholarship
They would be unable to find a
    suitable term
Worthy enough or strong enough to
    aptly describe your loveliness,
A word I know that has sufficiently
    fulfilled its duty,
In complimenting the sum of a man
    of your stature.

I dare not use the word *"good"*
To describe your love towards me,
For the application of an inadequate
    word
Would be an affront to you.

If ever I were to become an
    etymologist though,

Piérre Ramon Thomas

Just know that new adjectives—
Adjectives unheard of,
Adjectives unadulterated,
Words not yet sullied or carelessly
    uttered by deceitful lips—
Would be invented
And expressed only for you,
    My love.

If Only You Knew

So many boxes of Kleenex I went
    through before you came;
My head was a perpetual fountain
    from which water never ceased
    flowing.
Too weak and unable to utter words,
    my soul begged and pleaded God,
To bless me with someone to love,
    someone to hold.
Not granted my heart's desire,
The Great Spirit wrapped me in the
    blanket of His comfort on
    numerous occasions.

Your arrival into my life is cause for
    celebration,
Your presence, a gift from the
    universe;
Being reckless with your heart
Would be equivalent to me hawk-
    spitting in the face of my God.
That's why I've encased your heart in
    a see-through glass carrier
In the unlikely moment I forget to be
    kind to your delicate vulnerability.

My love, I carry you with me wherever
    I go.
        My love, I carry you with me wherever I go.
                My love, I carry you with me wherever I go.
                        My love, I carry you with me wherever I go.

Piérre Ramon Thomas

My love, I carry you with me wherever I go.

The Nomadic Poet

Send This Letter to My Lover, O Bird of the Air

Meet me in the night hours.
When our love is not at risk for
    judgment.
Be assured though, I am not ashamed
    of you.
How can a musician be ashamed of
    his instrument?
Yes,
I am the musician. You, my
    instrument;
Together we create majestic
    symphony.
I will anticipate you, keeping watch
    upon my balcony,
Donning the silk garment you love.
I will fragrance myself with oils of
    sandalwood and lavender
That I may intoxicate you upon
    arrival.
When this letter reaches you,
Go down to the market.
Purchase the wine and the fruit;
Petals and candles are awaiting you in
    my domain.

Ah! I just imagined my skin caressing
    your skin.
Briefly my body and mind went
    sweetly insane.

Piérre Ramon Thomas

Let me end this letter
That I may send it to you.
The quicker I send my words to you,
The quicker you may come to me.

Blown to Smithereens

A rather clumsy criminal he was.
I cautioned him,
"Lip-prints of your kisses
You have left as evidence all over me
Will give you away
Once you have ended my life."
He was rabid
Because the clouds of our fragrances
Blended together
Creating a new scent that induced
    insanity in him.

So, farewell world.
This is my swan song.
I, your humble rhymester and proser,
    am but no more.
The only enduring remnants of me
Are the smoldering bits of my flesh
    left around our bed.
My love, the top bomb expert in the
    world,
Has detonated me, blown me to
    smithereens.
So disoriented he has left me,
I no longer remember my name—
François? Yves? Laurent?—
Shoot! I know it's a French name!

Do me a favor, will you?

Piérre Ramon Thomas

Gather all the little pieces of me and
    place them in a casket of
    varnished oak.
At my funeral, let the choir sing Color
    Me Badd's "I Wanna Sex You
    Up"
And let my handsome murderer
    deliver my eulogy.

MY LOVER HAS PLEASURED
MY BODY UNTIL I
COULDN'T TAKE IT
ANYMORE

— This is what it reads on the walls
    of my mausoleum.

They Say

They say our love is too much,
Too performative.
They say our love is unhealthy:
We're way too into each other, overly
    and unnecessarily affectionate.
They say we're overcompensating:
Since our love has no substance, we're
    trying to prove something to
    ourselves.
They say our union will not last:
We burned so bright in the beginning,
    eventually, we'll burn out, go cold.
They say our love is unnatural:
A love like ours shouldn't be.

If they knew how long I had to mourn
    my loneliness,
They'd either rejoice with us or leave
    us alone.
If they knew how many windows I
    pressed my nose against,
Watching other couples in love,
    watching people enjoy their
    partners,
They'd let us be.
If they could witness all the tally
    marks on my bedroom walls,
The numbered days of my loneliness,
The humanity within them would
    bless our union.

Piérre Ramon Thomas

So what if you are my medicine,
And frequently I overdose on you—
How does my well-being affect them?

Maybe they are just jealous,
That the kind of love we have is
    nonexistent between them and
    their partners;
They wish they could have what we
    have
Yet despise us because we found
    something special in a time like
    this.

Or,
Maybe they're angry we're not
    ashamed of our love,
We don't take pains to hide our
    affections in the dark or behind
    closed doors.

Cause & Effect

The effect the lights of a chandelier
Has on a diamond necklace worn on
    the neck of a woman
To make it glitter and sparkle,
Is the same exact effect you and your
    love have on me.
The effects of you and your love are
    not mutually exclusive,
I cannot tell either of them apart;
The very presence of you, here, is an
    indication of your love,
And your sweetness, your love in
    action, is an exhibition, an exposé
    of you.
If, in regard to love, my heart is
    likened to a seed,
Then you are my sunlight, my rain, my
    soil, my air.
And my heart doesn't just grow,
The foliage that grows is a
    representation of how tenderly,
    how attentively you love me.
I visit lakes and ponds and creeks after
    heavy rains,
For they are the only things on God's
    green Earth
That can relate to how I feel
After you have poured your affections
    upon me.

Piérre Ramon Thomas

The Definition of Poetry

This is poetry:
You and I lying here together,
Naked,
Our unclothed bodies blending into
    one another,
Our souls dancing, moving in circles
    at some place in the universe,
Our sensations being erratic,
Our perfectly coordinated touches and
    soft massages—
Mmm.

The type of poetry I wish to recite
    every day.

Finally

Out of the darkness in which I was imprisoned,

Details of your face came into being;

Imagined outlines, contours, and pigmentation of your form

Became solid, physical matter.

Simultaneously, light was born

Decreeing you as its originator

And that luminance is not conceived of the sun,

Nor the moon,

Not even the stars;

They are just mere reflectors of *your* brilliance.

Your sweet breath, upon which my being clings,

Are gaseous airs the Supreme One codified

Into the laws of nature:

A Divine Communion between humans and plants.

Piérre Ramon Thomas

Your height, my bear, can now be measured numerically, in centimeters

And not by the metric of fairies, leprechauns or cyclopes;

Your mass, physicists can now measure in kilograms

And not by libraries of poetry.

Pining Away

All I need is for you to look in my
   direction,
See me eyeing your silhouette.
Imagine, a second, a lifetime of my
   affection,
Let us gamble on this duet.
Consider me, of all your options of
   men,
Even though I am not as flawless;
I will take you on a journey with no
   end,
Render love to you in its rawness.
O how, for you, I pine,
Moping, sighing every hour,
I pray persistently for you to be mine
That I may surrender to your power.
By your eyes, I am entranced.
By your smile, I am taken.
By your voice, my ears dance.
By your presence, I am awakened.
If you knew how deep my fantasies
   went,
Of one thing you would be assured in
   life:
Love's objective is appeasement
Uprooting seeds of doubt which may
   bring strife.
I wonder if you sit and dream,
In the same manner as I;

Piérre Ramon Thomas

I could only hope your countenance
    beams
Upon thoughts of me passing by.
When time comes for you to answer
    'yea' or 'nay',
I hope you will be kindhearted;
I hope I have sparked a fire in you
    today
Because you already had mine started.

THE TIE THAT BINDS

The Contents of This Wooden Box

From you, all I received was a wooden box
And I could fit all of the *"I love yous"*,
The one or two hugs I received from you,
Those couple of kisses you gave me
Into that one, small wooden box…
And guess what?
I still have much room in that wooden box left.
And I suppose to believe you love me?

Over the years, my wooden box cried to you for more—
More articles,
But my wooden box went neglected.
I want you to understand I had to live off of those few articles,
For many suns and many moons.
Now my wooden box wants nothing from you;
It spits out whatever you attempt to put in.
No, my wooden box isn't unforgiving
But I will admit it is warped from salty water.[47]
Now that this wooden box is out of your possession, you want to invest in it;

Piérre Ramon Thomas

You open it hoping to find diamonds
 and silver.
To your surprise you find nickel and
 lint and cobwebs.
But I can only present to you what
 you have placed on its splintered
 lining.

In contrast, I received a treasury,
A treasury full of emeralds and rubies
 and sapphires!
My treasury is filled to the brim with
 all of the kisses,
All of the hugs,
All of the pride,
Every last "I love you"
My grandparents ever gave to me.

The Unloved Son

Under the regime of my mother,
The supplies of her affection and
    comfort were withheld from me.
Her abuse and punishments were
    ever-present like a best friend
But her tenderness or praise, as
    frequent as Halley's Comet.
Due to that emotional negligence,
I sought for validation in others.

Yet nothing is given for free;
Something is always expected,
    exchanged in return.
Full-grown men whispered sweet-
    nothings in my ear,
Telling me how pretty I was or how
    they wanted to show their desires
    for me.
But what a high price I had to pay,
To hear those things and to keep
    them near.

Easy it is *not* to overhaul the mind.
Through daily affirmations,
I had to tell myself
And convince myself
Of all the things I wanted to believe
    about myself.

But oh how green the grass is now

Piérre Ramon Thomas

In the land in which I dwell!
How cottony-soft the clouds are here
That decorate clear blue skies!
Here, I am not a poor man begging
    others to sustain me;[48]
I am a well-to-do man with wealth
    gained from my own hard work.[49]

The Significance of a Father

If my father was present in my
    existence from birth,
Where, in life, would I have been?

Would I have possessed the same
    gauge of strength?
Or would it be more…
    Or less?

Would I have had a better relationship
    with my mother?
Would I have treated my siblings
    better?
Sometimes I wonder what my life
    would have been like if he was
    there.

Would I have felt the need to keep
    searching,
Remaining restless in my soul—
Just running all the time?

Would I understand myself better,
Why I do the things I do?

If my father was present in my life,
Like he should've been,
I wouldn't have had to keep jumping
    from house to house
When I was homeless.

Piérre Ramon Thomas

I wonder, if my father was present and
    accounted for,
Would I have discovered my talents
    earlier?
Would he have drawn my gift out to
    surface,
So that I would've had ample time to
    hone it?

Would my mind have been a little
    sharper?
And my thoughts a little clearer?
Would I have still struggled with that
    image which reflected in the
    mirror?

Would he have avenged me
When my mother's husband abused
    me?
Would he have been my voice
When my voice wasn't yet developed?

All of the wisdom he could've
    invested in me,
Supposed to invest in me,
Is floating arbitrarily in the air out
    there,
Never to settle on my ears.

The massive treasury of hugs and
    kisses and *"I love yous"*
Which he was obligated to give me,
Is an empty, condemned building

Now that he is gone.

Just as you are buried "father",
I want to bury my memories and
    feelings of you.

Piérre Ramon Thomas

Louis

At the age of five and unaware
Of your needy soul,
Hugging every man you meet,
Taking their laps as your seat,
A father is what you were owed.

Yet you were cheated, little Louis,
Neglected, of a paternal touch.
He did not acknowledge the
    significance
Of your existence,
Being there was just too much.

You are not alone, be comforted,
It happened to most of us
Who went without the hugs
Or the head rubs
From the man whose love was a must.

Louis, Louis, little one,
Getting attached to male friends of
    your mother.
Saying "I love you" without
    apprehension,
My tears get your attention
Because you are what I am layers-
    uncovered.

Your soul is evident, young one,
All the spectators see

The Nomadic Poet

That what you desire
Is to be hoisted higher
On your father's shoulders or
    bounced upon his knee.

Louis, Louis, little boy,
Sprouting without a father;
Inside I look like you,
Rather we all do,
Whose fathers willingly departed.

Piérre Ramon Thomas

Which Wire Do I Cut?

How unfair
That the both
Of you
Constructed a bomb,
Yet I am the one
Left with the responsibility
Of defusing myself
So that I
Would not be
A terrorist
To others.

A Letter to the Children I May Never Have

(Inspired by "Song for the Baby" by Kelis)

To my lovely son and precious daughter,

Forgive me.

I really wanted to bring you into this world, but I refuse to bring you into this messy life and force you to endure the pain and heartache and cruelty that is waiting to pounce on you. I would be remiss if I did not acknowledge that there is *some* good present in this world; there is a remnant of people who are keeping the concept of love alive.

I didn't have the best of parents: my father abandoned me, choosing not to be in my life; and my mother was *very* cold, distant, abusive, and unaffectionate. Due to the parents I had and how they chose to wield their responsibility for me, I am left severely inadequate. Even to this day, I am still dealing with the physical and emotional trauma of what they've done and said to me. I fear that I would not be enough for you. Moreover, I would never—*never* forgive myself if I were to traumatize you like my parents did to me. And so, for that, now is not the time to bring you into this world, if I choose to bring you into this world at all. I am still healing. Still. I do not wish to burden you with the baggage I carry. It would be my responsibility to ensure that the demons I battle do not visit you. I know I would never abandon the both of you for I am not some pathetic, piss-poor excuse of a man, but I do fear that I would try to overcompensate; I would try to make up for all the love and affection I didn't receive and I don't want to smother you. Smothering you would not be good either.

There are men—there are even women now—who prey on little children. Yes, my little rugrats, there are sickos in this world. I have had *too many* family members and friends who've told me so. What good would I be to you if I were in prison? Why would I be in prison you ask? I would kill them. Man or woman, whomever touches you or violates you or robs you of your innocence, I would kill them. I was not made to be a murderer and have never murdered anyone in my entire life but...I don't think that the Earth has enough water to extinguish the fire of my fury if ever you were to tell me that someone has violated you. May God have mercy on the perverted, sick soul who would dare light that fire.

Son, the rules of masculinity are too rigid at this present time. Although I would teach you that it's okay to express your feelings or to cry or to be sensitive, the world would not reinforce what I teach. You would hear one doctrine at home, then, an entirely different doctrine—actually, a heresy—from the world, and you might struggle inside yourself as to which one is right. Even though you might love me and want to make me proud, the women you may pursue, would not like the doctrine that I taught you, thinking you to be weak or too sensitive. The men you may seek to befriend, will accuse you of being gay and in order to fit in with them, you might conform. I do not want that for you. I would also want you to respect women. Not because you have a sister, or that one day you may have a daughter, but I would want you to respect women because it's simply the right thing to do. The world doesn't adhere to this sound doctrine, so...

Daughter, the world has made you their enemy. I cannot even thoroughly list all the struggles you would fight for I, being a man, do not encounter a fraction of the troubles women are vexed with—especially black women. Women's bodies are policed in a way that men's bodies are not. Your "no" isn't respected. Women *still* don't get equal pay for equal work. How can I bring you here when this may be your reality?

Finally, to my shame and embarrassment, I am poor. I cannot bring you here only to suffer lack. I know what it is like to grow up poor. The shame. The inability to ask for your heart's desires. Now, I wouldn't spoil you, but I definitely wouldn't want you to know hunger or homelessness either.

If any part of this letter is stained or blurry, it's because of my tears: I was crying while I was writing this. Even though you do not exist yet, I love you. And because I love you, I cannot force you to endure this. At least not yet. Maybe.

Forgive me. Forgive me, my little rugrats.

Your dad,
Pop-Pop

MUSINGS

MUSING I

People *say* that they love deeply, only to give up or find comfort in another's arms at the *first* sign of trouble.

MUSING II

Respect is not important to you
If you yourself are disrespectful.

MUSING III

Binary thinking cannot be applied to every concept, every idea, every subject; some things, in most cases, most things, require nuance—nuanced critical analysis.

MUSING IV

It is impossible to be offended by others
If you do not care what others think.

MUSING V

Divorce is so common nowadays that I no longer get excited when I hear about people getting engaged or married; I get excited when I hear of their years together.

MUSING VI

Piérre Ramon Thomas

How frustrating it is to be a respectful person in a time when the principles of respect and civility are rare and opted out for contempt.

MUSING VII

There are an infinite number of ways to respond to a situation, but the *right* way numbers somewhere around one.

MUSING VIII

When it comes to blame,
I am blind and in a land all by myself.

MUSING IX

Beauty only indicates beauty;
It does not allude to moral character.

MUSING X

I have never lived by that ignorant notion of "respect is earned, not given". Who am I for you to earn my respect? Who are you that I must earn your respect?

Rather, I live by the philosophy that respect is given and not earned. It is given simply because you are a human being: the same elements that constitute me, are within you.

Now, to *maintain* my respect is solely, entirely, utterly up to you and how *you* choose to treat me.

MUSING XI

~~"Men are logical. Women are emotional."~~

This sentiment is shortsighted, limiting, and doesn't capture the complexity and uniqueness of human beings. Some women are more logical. Some men are more emotional. For the most part, we're all different proportions of both.

MUSING XII

If you can't pay someone a compliment—when one is undeniably due—you are either threatened by them or you're just mean-spirited.

MUSING XIII

There's nothing wrong with speaking first, texting first, saying "I love you" first, giving first.

But this egotistical, self-centered time that we're living in will tell you to not be vulnerable until a person is vulnerable with you first.

This is why most of us are lonely and unhappy now.

MUSING XIV

With any social relationship, both parties *have* to contribute to building it, whether they may be associates, acquaintances, companions, buddies, pals, friends, close friends, best friends, soulmates, significant others, partners, fiancés, spouses, and, last but not least, family members (children excluded).

For example: I give a little, you give a little; you give a little, I give a little. This cycle continues until the relationship is established and both parties know that both have contributed equally to the establishment of the relationship. No party should be expected to give so much first before anything is given in return. (Even so much as saying "hi" is too much for some because they don't want to appear desperate, vulnerable, or for it to be said that they were "pressed" for the other.)

On the other hand, if only one person in the relationship is giving and not receiving anything in return, they should STOP GIVING. That person should sit back and see if they will be rewarded with the measure that they gave out. (How painful it is to give love and not see the other party make even a little bit of an effort to give love back.)

The moral of the story is this in a nutshell: Give. Don't be scared to give first. But, if you don't see a return, wash your hands, walk away and don't look back.

MUSING XV

The world has become so cynical, so pessimistic, so negative, that people either expect the worse from you before they get to know you, or they start off not liking you until you give them a reason to like you.

MUSING XVI

Building friendships, although requires work, should not be forced. They should develop organically.

MUSING XVII

Asking questions is one of the signs of intelligence because only a fool would conclude that his assumptions were facts and truth.

MUSING XVIII

A young man once asked his mother, "Why don't you hug us and kiss us and tell us 'I love you'?" The mother twisted up her face and nastily replied, "Y'all don't do it to me!"

It is never the responsibility of the child to establish an affectionate relationship with their parents. Never. It is the role, the duty, the obligation of the parents to establish an affectionate relationship with their children. It is erroneous and ignorant to think otherwise.

Once a parent establishes an affectionate relationship with their child, the child learns how to reciprocate that affection back to their parents, and they are better equipped to be affectionate toward others.

MUSING XIX

Piérre Ramon Thomas

You cannot kill the humanity in a little boy, then, expect him to be humane or sympathetic to others when he becomes a man.

MUSING XX

Men, if no one else told you: It's okay to be sensitive, it's okay to cry, and you aren't less of a man for feeling or expressing emotions.

MUSING XXI
(At Shenandoah National Park)

I was unaware of the pride in my heart
Until the grandeur of nature was juxtaposed to small me.

MUSING XXII

Every time I say I'm happy, something always happens to grieve me.

Maybe I need not acknowledge my happiness out loud, to prevent the demons of depression from afflicting me and disrupting said happiness.

MUSING XXIII

I am leery of "spiritual men" and "spiritual women" who don't teach from their own mistakes and life lessons. There is much more sage wisdom from the teaching from one's mistakes than from the regurgitation of "spiritual knowledge" one has learned from the lips of someone else or from a book.

MUSING XXIV

I love when people misread me because it lets me know that they're either illiterate or they did not have the desire or patience to get to know me. I want no company with either of those type of individuals.

MUSING XXV

It is not my responsibility to persuade or dissuade someone concerning their opinion of me. Whatever a person thinks of me is their truth. And who am I to challenge someone's truth?

MUSING XXVI

It is futile to be offended when someone doesn't speak, when you also have a mouth that can do the same. It is not a sign of weakness, your world will not collapse, nor will you bleed to death if you speak first. If you find yourself getting offended because someone doesn't speak to you:

OPEN YOUR MOUTH AND SPEAK

MUSING XXVII

How very dangerous it is for a child to rely on others who aren't his family to build his self-esteem and convince him he's loved.

MUSING XXVIII

Whether you say something or nothing, your actions or inactions speak for you. And whatever that person hears is their interpretation of what you said in the absence or presence of your words.

MUSING XXIX

Please! For the love of all that is good and holy, do not "comfort" someone whose mother wasn't a good mother with the insensitive words of "Well, cherish her still; you only get one mother".

Not every person was blessed with a good mother. As much as it pains me to say this, not every mother deserves honor!

MUSING XXX

It's hard when us paupers get money because we're making up for all the times that we *severely* needed or *desperately* wanted something and were unable to get it. Sensible financial management should be our aspiration though.

MUSING XXXI

Do not expect from someone else
What you yourself are not willing to give.

MUSING XXXII

I have been so engrossed in my education from books that I have neglected one of the most important educations of all: *education from nature*. I have restricted myself from communicating with nature so much that I have lost the knowledge of the nature of Nature and how to properly commune with her. But Nature is forgiving though, for once I determine within myself to spend time with her, she opens wide her arms and encloses me within them.

MUSING XXXIII

Pineapples go on pizza. Preferably with chicken. Case closed. ☺

MUSING XXXIV

Humankind is one community; humans are not islands unto themselves. What affects one, affects us all. We benefit from the success of one and we feel the effects of the failure and suffering of one. We have a responsibility towards our fellow human being. Whatever is in our power to do, we should strive to do.

MUSING XXXV

Compassion is one trait that is capable of touching *every* aspect of human interaction.

MUSING XXXVI

It costs $0.00 to be kind.

And it takes less than 5 seconds to say: "Please", "Thank You", "Excuse Me", or "I'm Sorry".

Piérre Ramon Thomas

MUSING XXXVII

Strive for balance. Balance and moderation.

MUSING XXXVIII

Gold unearthed is a sad, pitiful thing,
And for her to lack a digger is a shame and a tragedy.

MUSING XXXIX

Me loving you does not absolve you from being wrong. Although I may love you, I can—and will—still call you out when you're wrong.

MUSING XL

To a negative person,
Even positive things can be critiqued negatively.

MUSING XLI

I am everything and I am nothing.

I am important and I am insignificant.

I am somebody and I am nobody.

All at once.

MUSING XLII

Knowledge is king, Wisdom is queen;

They are the only monarchy I recognize.

MUSING XLIII

Lips tell lies
But the eyes are truth-tellers.

MUSING XLIV

Even if there are 100 members of a group and you meet 99 members of said group, *still* you cannot make assumptions about all 100 members of that group.

Human beings are individuals. Complex individuals. It is small-minded to make assumptions—even if they are "positive" assumptions—about a member of a group of people, about a *human being*, because you first experience them as a stereotype.

Then, when you observe their uniqueness, their individuality, then and only then are your preconceived notions dismantled. Essentially, you rob that person of you experiencing them in and of themselves[50] without any frames of reference or prior negative models.

MUSING XLV

It's okay to learn before you do. It's okay to be an apprentice first. It's okay to wait until it's your time.

MUSING XLVI

~~To feel is feminine.~~

Piérre Ramon Thomas

To feel is human.

MUSING XLVII

I will not subject the content of my literature to the times; the times will subject itself to the content of my literature.

MUSING XLVIII

Majority of women only want gay men as lap dogs, show dogs to perform tricks.

It was said that, "When gay men have women as their best friends, those women have other women as their best friends."

It appears that women don't actually want gay men as friends in the true sense but as archetypical playthings:
The Makeup Maven Friend,
The Hairdresser Friend,
The Fashionista Friend,
The Mean Girl Friend,
The Town Gossip Friend,
The Comic Relief Friend,
The D.L. Bloodhound Friend,
Or, The Let's-Get-Drunk-And-Go-Dancing Friend.

I cannot be anyone's entertainment. I cannot be a form of someone's amusement. The friendships I forge must be substantive. If we can't cry together and get to know each other intimately, we won't laugh and dance together.

MUSING XLIX

Expelling a human being from your uterus, does not make you a mother. What makes a woman a mother is how she carries out and fulfills her maternal duties. Any woman can be an egg donor, but only a select few are *mothers*.

True feminism—true, principled, non-hypocritical feminism would give space to children, especially adult children, to express or vent their grievances against their mothers, if their mothers were, in fact, un-motherly or abusive or cold or distant or unaffectionate.

More often than not, when people complain about deadbeat dads, absentee fathers or abusive, un-fatherly fathers, no one—NO ONE—silences them by saying, "Cherish him still. You only get one father."

But when a person expresses their grievances, *legitimate grievances*, about their mother, almost instantaneously do they get silenced with the inhumane, dismissive statement of, "Cherish her. Honor her still. You only get one mother."

MUSING L

I am jealous of uncomplicated people,
Of their easy-breeziness,

Piérre Ramon Thomas

Of their openness like unencumbered land.

Because, conversely, I am a labyrinth:
A complicated series of high walls, dead ends,
And secret passageways.
Me: crestfallen at the center.

IF THEY SAY WHY? WHY?—TELL 'EM THAT IT'S HUMAN NATURE

The Masked Woman

She, like many others, climbs out of bed,
Pins her hair back,
And puts on the finest threads ever sewn.
Before leaving her dwelling she picks up the mask from her dresser,
Fastens it to her face.
Her ugly visage testifies of the years of pain and abuse she has endured
But everyone wants her to always exhibit a blissful air.
She can never reveal her true face
Because. the one time she mistakenly did, people were offended.
Do not think that in the presence of laughter,
There is an absence of sorrow.
The masked woman, behind her hearty chuckles,
Is being whipped and abused by her husband at home.
He drags her across the floor by her hair,
He spits on her and slaps her until he imprints a mark upon her cheek.
He kicks her in the back and stomach with his boots still on.
He belittles her saying, "Nobody wants you!"

Piérre Ramon Thomas

Every morning, she turns on the
    charm again,
Mask fixated upon her face,
And no one knows the difference.

I Have Yet to See

(Inspired by "For You I Will" by Monica and "Breaking the Law" by Emeli Sandé)

I have yet to see the stars plucked out
    of the sky
Or all the flowers collected from every
    garden and every field
Or the sun and moon given to an
    individual
Or one cross oceans and rivers
Or one traverse the ends of the Earth
All for the sake of love.
Yet, people come together promising
    these very things
And people break apart and these
    feelings are gone.

Instead of making promises of grand
    proportions,
Guarantee the realistic, the tangible,
    the things within your finite
    capabilities.
Promise sincere, deep adoration
All the days of your short life.
Promise heartfelt appreciation
For the little things as well as the
    noticeable things.
Promise you will work through the
    fights and the screams
With all your strength to salvage what
    you have.

Piérre Ramon Thomas

Promise you will be blind to everyone
    else
And only have sight for one.
Promise you will massage their feet
If their feet ached from working all
    day.
Promise you will buy or prepare
Whatever food they're craving.
Promise they will have a safe place,
    free of judgment,
In your arms when they cry.
Promise you will laugh with them.
Promise you will dance with them.
Promise that, no, you will not run
But fight battles and wage wars
    together, side by side.
Guarantee them all the hugs and all
    the kisses
Their lovely hearts could possibly
    desire.

After you do all of that,
    And only after,
Then can you promise them the
    world.

Give Love Longevity

Love's intention has been eternity
Since the beginning of time.
Nowadays,
People have cut love's time short
To just brief encounters in the
 bedroom.
Love is supposed to extend beyond
Nights of passion.

Piérre Ramon Thomas

The Hills of Towoldji

(A Poetic Tale)

I looked off into the distance and saw
A picturesque field
Of healthy,
Finely-trimmed,
Vibrant
Green grass.
And the flowers—*oh the flowers*!
The flowers of the gardens of this
    field,
Was as if a gardener took his time
And carefully colored each petal with
    a paintbrush.
As is my custom, I began wandering
    around
Exploring the extents of the field.
I bent down and put my nose to the
    flowers
Unafraid of the chance of being stung
    by a bee.
I carried on with my hike through
    paradise and proceeded to ascend
    up a hill;
It was not until I reached the highest
    plateau that I halted to take in the
    view.
The arrangement of the clouds in the
    sky, set against the hills in the
    distance,

The Nomadic Poet

Made me feel unworthy to set my
    sight to such a wondrous view.
Below me laid a depression in the
    midst of the hills
Which was occupied with a patio
    constructed of marble.
Upon one of the eight benches on the
    patio sat a young, virgin woman
Of poise, grace, and unparalleled
    beauty.
This swan of a woman twirled her
    fingers in her hair
And smiled as if she thought pleasant
    thoughts.
Meeting her, walking onto the patio,
    was a young, virgin man
Who possessed the world's most
    delicate, gentle heart.
The young woman arose to greet the
    gleeful young man,
Wrapping her arms around him.
Following their long embrace,
He took her chocolate brown hands
    and brought them to his lips,
Kissing them longingly.
The young woman's smile could not
    be hidden nor did she want to
    stifle it;
Vulnerability was their aspiration,
    transparency their intention.
The young man sat her upon the
    bench and whispered beautiful
    lyrics to her.

Piérre Ramon Thomas

I could hear everything the gentleman
    said to the lady,
But I dare not share the private things
    he declared to her.

After observing all this, sorrow
    overtook me,
Settling down to the bones in my
    body.
I plopped to the ground
For my knees became weak and
    buckled from overwhelming
    sadness.

My mind knew that in my era, in my
    lifetime, love like this,
Deep, uninhibited love, does not exist.

Worsening the matter was that *I*
    would never experience a love like
    that.
Because
I live in *this* era.
Therefore, *I* will never find deep,
    uninhibited love.

The Nomadic Poet

Let Words Mean What They Say They Mean

Poor word, you've lost your breadth:
You no longer mean what you were
    meant to mean.
If one were to utter you
You would not be taken seriously.
Due to abuse and overuse,
The vibrancy you held
And the freshness you contained
Is like a vague dream now.

Feeble word, I cry out for you
For you cannot stand up for yourself.
I aspire to preserve your beauty
Before it is too late.

Blessed word, you will always be
    defined to me,
Worry not about your admirer;
Know that I will ever pour and not
    sputter
Unlike those who regard you not.

Lovely word, make your nest
Upon my tongue.
Let our affair remain throughout time.
I've planted forget-me-nots to remind
    me of you.
I will not be like those who speak
    many things
But say nothing

Piérre Ramon Thomas

Nor like those who don't say enough
When more is necessary.
Believe that I will do you justice
In a world where you are continuously
    assaulted.

Multiplicity Theorem

A firecracker is inert until it is lit;
It is erroneous to believe that it is
   always shooting off.
No.
Most of the time, the explosive is
   sitting quietly on the shelf,
Minding its own business,
And then along comes someone who
   brings fire,
      Some incendiary busybody,
And activates the explosive.

One is really many;
At the same time, many are one.
One is *not* one;
And many are *not* many.[51]

Piérre Ramon Thomas

The Three Hardest Words to Say

The three hardest words to say,
And possibly the most difficult phrase
    in any language,
Is not "I LOVE YOU":
Even the most conniving and
    deceitful can utter those words.
But what the bullheaded cannot say,
What their lips forbid them from
    saying
Is, "I WAS WRONG."

Star-Struck

Awe of a celebrity is more so elation,
An exuberant applause from the soul,
At the talent of the individual
As opposed to the conduit herself.

Piérre Ramon Thomas

Light

It is important to note
That just a little bit of light from a
    candle
Pushes back the darkness
Providing a circumference of
    luminance for the candleholder
    the darkness cannot overpower.
The greater the light,
The lesser the darkness.

Processed Food

I don't want your processed food;[52]
My belly rejects it because it lacks
 nutrition.
Your food is filled with synthetic
 preservatives,
Artificial flavorings, colors,
And unnecessary additives
To enhance its edibleness.
I, myself, am a food-from-the-earth
 man:
I consume the vegetables, for they're
 filled with minerals and vitamins;
I consume the meat, for the protein it
 contains;
I consume the fruits, for its
 antioxidants and natural sugars;
I consume the grains, for the fiber
 that they supply;
And I utilize the herbs for their
 medicinal properties.

I challenge you to regurgitate and
 denounce
Processed food you were force-fed
 from youth.
If you're protruding and getting fat
And your health is declining,
Demand and search for food with
 substance

Piérre Ramon Thomas

So cancer and hypertension and heart
disease will not claim your life.

High Standards

I crave a lover who,
After pleasuring my body,
Will pleasure my mind with knowledge,
Feeding my soul with nuggets of deep musings.

That would be a lover!

Piérre Ramon Thomas

Where Are the Colors in Your Words?

Gray.
Gray is the color of your words
Since you mean not what you say.
When you were a child,
Colors filled your words;
When you had opened your mouth,
One would witness a rainbow.
Sometimes, words passing your lips
    are radiant
Only to lose their hue when you don't
    fulfill the guarantees you've made.
At other times, you could keep your
    statements to yourself
Since they were lackluster from the
    origin of its thought.
Where are the colors in your words?
Where are the *colors* in your words?
Where are the colors in your *words*?
Walk with me
And say not three words.
So when you, at least, say one,
I would be ecstatic over the color of
    that one.

The Romantic Who Doesn't Romanticize Love

Some men call him delusional
Because he dreams of love everlasting;
But, he's not as starry-eyed as one
    might think:
He welcomes the storms but
    anticipates their passing.
He is well aware love is riddled
With bickering and sorrows;
All hardships he would gladly accept
If it means having neverending
    tomorrows.
He says, "Love is not always easy.
It requires constant work to keep the
    heart stirred.
Fights and tears are destined to come,
Yet perseverance will save if *'love'* is
    the word."

Piérre Ramon Thomas

How Does It Feel to Be God's Favorites?

If you happen to find yourself
Seated comfortably among the
    beautiful, unburdened, beloved
    elite,
The fortunate few who've found their
    significant others,
Consider yourself blessed you have
    escaped the petty monotony that
    constitutes modern dating.

Doesn't it feel wonderful to know
That he or she whom you text
Will text you back?
And although intercourse is
    pleasurable and explosive,
Doesn't it feel good to go out...

        ...in public...

                ...on a date?
Isn't just the mere assurance of
    reciprocity pure bliss,
Living in a world where the love you
    measure out
Is measured back to you?
Isn't the proclamation—*the act of
    someone publicly claiming you*—
Enough to fill the boundaries of your
    heart with joy until there's no
    room left—

The Nomadic Poet

It spills over?!
Aren't you comforted knowing that
During your final days, someone will
    be there—or will have been
    there—
Depending?

Piérre Ramon Thomas

Be Mindful

How difficult it is—
Nay! Impossible, dare I say—
   To coax a newly freed bird back into his cage,
   To refill a pitcher with its recently spilled juice,
   Or to corral a barrage of hurtful words once
            they've passed the lips of a reckless
            individual.

Death to Cordiality!

At first, we exiled you
From our towns and cities.
But you were stubborn
So we resorted to extreme measures.
We took you by your neck with our hooks.
We dragged you through the dirt.
We whipped you mercilessly.
You were made a public example
To all who chose to follow you.
Finally, we beheaded you
To end your influence.
But wait!
There are some of your followers,
       Cordiality,
Hiding as refugees in our cities.
We will find them
And we will end them.

Piérre Ramon Thomas

I Am Not Psychic But...

If I,
Like a fortune teller,
Cannot look into
The orb of your eye
And see forever,

Silver-and-purple-glittered visions
Of the two of us
Growing old together,
Crow's feet and smile lines from excessive laughter,

Hazy, dream-like episodes,
Of in-the-backseat-of-the-car
Or hotel-balcony sex—
Numerous scenes of moans, grunts, and thrusts,

If I can't foresee
Warmly saturated pictures
Of our trips to
London, Italy, and France:
Selfies at Buckingham Palace,
    In front of the Trevi Fountain,
        And underneath the Arc de Triomphe,

Then,
It is not
In the cards—
Nor the stars—
For us.

Every Heart Deserves Love

One should not have to ask for the
    display of someone's love;
It should be given before it is needed.
The debtor needs not look within his
    pockets to pay the debt of love
For the payment is not in the coins or
    the bills:
It is found in his heart.
The heart is where love is stored up
But some lock away their affections
Only to neglect those who come
    looking for their portion.
That's why many are wandering
    through alleyways and gutters,
With bowls extended,
Searching for someone, *anyone*, to fill
    them.

POETRY ABOUT POETRY

Verbal Orgasms

The cornucopia of words that exist
And all the possibilities of
The arrangement of those words
Arouse me—
Mentally.
Intoxicated from wordlust,
I have no choice but to
Release all pent-up energy,
Weaving words together,
Meticulously selecting the most
    adequate of words
To convey my most innermost
    feelings
Until I keel over,
Panting heavily from a mixture of
Exhaustion, delight, and pleasure.

Piérre Ramon Thomas

The Curse of Love Poets

I, myself:
A relic.
My art upon these here scrolls:
Literature misplaced in time.
My scratches and squiggles:
Words of a dead subject.
There exists not even one literary
    archeologist
Or expert translator—

My words are nothing but
Mumblings to an audience of none.

Restraining Myself from Poetry

I haven't yet sold myself to poetry
For I am seized by apprehensive hesitation.
(I am fearful of what'll spring up from the depths of me).
While I desire to never cease producing pieces,
Others seem to effortlessly bring forth marvelous words.

May it be, I pray,
That the spirit of poetry,
Which has been since the beginning of time,
Fall on me
So I may pour forth riddles and rhymes,
Enigmas and parables,
Dark sayings and proverbs.
O that I may learn synchronicity with the poetic spirit
So that I may compose compositions like a composer,
Write writings like a writer,
Prophesy prophecies like a prophet.

Currently, I limit myself
Not allowing letters and words to have their way with me.
I seal up treasures of wisdom

Piérre Ramon Thomas

And cast them back into the sea.
My soul is not yet given…
    …dipped…
    …coated…
    …permeated…
In that which is poetry.

Yet.

Out of Words He Created Me

At the genesis of my formation,
When energies collided and my form
    stretched and ached into being,
He took the letters and words of my
    mother's tongue,
Shaped the zygote that would become
    all the future versions of myself.
In His infinite wisdom,
He turned that cell-shaped outline of
    letters
Into bone, blood, muscles and tissue;
Words that I have not yet discovered,
Occupy all atoms within my body.

When I wrote my first poem,[53]
Words were skipping down my arm,
Leaping, diving from my fingertips,
Bleeding onto the page.

It all started as a love affair:
I married myself to words;
I took it upon myself to become the
    Guardsman:
Preserver of the chastity of written
    and oral expressions.

Hearing particular words induced
    visions,
Visions that gave birth to tall tales.

Piérre Ramon Thomas

Feelings, like the juice of grapes, aged
 within my heart's cellar
Into alcoholic wine of emotional
 diatribes.
The poetic spirit whispered utterances
My ear was primed to hear.

As this mountain erodes,
Fragments of words come tumbling
 down,
In avalanches, until I am pebbles,
Gravel, and then dust.

A Religion Unto Itself

(First published in Marymount University's 2021
Literary Arts Magazine *BlueInk*)

How solemn and sacred it is
For a man to consecrate his time
And regard the rantings or ravings,
Musings or fancies
Of a poet.

Such a noble sacrifice of self
To make still one's soul
And give attention to the labor
Of thoughtful, careful composition
And arrangement of words
Of a rhymer or proser.

The liturgical acts of: attending
The high-steepled cathedral,
The rain-stained temple,[54]
Constructed from deep ruminations;
    Gazing upon the stained-glass windows
    Of fracted, colorful images
    Conjured up and imagined
    By the pope of literary art;
        Listening with the ears
        Of the heart and mind
        To the poetic and prosaic scriptures
        Of the gospel of the anointed wordsmith;
All are devotions done by the reader
For baptism in the doctrine of his
    verses.

Piérre Ramon Thomas

Sympathy—*even up to empathy*—
Is tithed
Into the collection plate of the poet
That the reader causes herself
To partake in his thoughts, emotions,
    and feelings
Wheresoever the good ones or the
    depressed ones
Had taken him.

The Nomadic Poet

The Poet's Burden

Why did You set these words within
    me,
Incinerating me from the inside until I
    have no choice but to expel them,
If people care not to take the time to
    read or listen
To the words I have labored to give
    birth to?

Singers open their mouths blowing
    melodious air
And listeners scream and cheer at the
    serenading of their ears;
Dancers twirl and spin, gliding over
    rhythm and beats
And others *ooh* and *aah* at the wonder
    of syncopation;
Instrumentalists pluck and blow,
    creating new sounds,
And others clap in awe of their
    musical ingenuity;
Tinkers map out and build items other
    men use
And the lives of those men are made
    easier by new technologies.

But poets write words that set fire to
    towns and cities
And nary a man cares to notice even
    the wood kindling under his feet.

Piérre Ramon Thomas

However, the fire we create seeks not
    to turn a man to ashes
But to engulf and consume him 'til he
    is purged, refined gold,
Emblaze his mind 'til he understands
    esoteric matters,
Enkindle his senses 'til his faculties are
    quickened and his raw passions
    articulated.

ENDNOTES

1 *holy temple of love...consecrated monastery...romantic church*

   These terms, in this composition, represents the heart

2 *Architect*

   God, the Creator of the edifice that is the heart

3 *one dedicated monk...high priest*

   These terms, in this composition, represent a lover, a significant other, a partner

4 *laypeople*

   Single people

5 *visiting priests*

   This term, in this composition, represents other people in love, other couples

6 *temple-keeper*

   This phrase, in this composition, represents the owner of the edifices which represent the heart

7   *undesirable men...sacrilegious hooligans...mob of careless gangsters*

        These phrases, in this composition, represent men who get involved with others under the pretense that their intentions are towards a relationship and/or men who ghost others

8   *To his dismay, all he was found was rubble, overturned statues and perpetual smoke rising from the ruins*

        Representing heartbreak and all unnecessary hurt inflicted by a partner; the aftermath of such heartbreak

9   *long stood cold*

        Going without affection, intimacy, or sexual relations for a *very*, *very* long time

10   *sun*

        When used in this context, represents affection, love, warmth, passion

11   *overcast*

        Represents depression, sadness, sorrow

12   *field...earth*

When used in this context, represents a person's body

13   *floods...creeks...tsunamis*

Represents crying at varying intensities

14   *the building*

In this composition, this term represents the heart

15   *fire*

Passion

16   *abandon...left it*

These phrases, in this composition, represent men who get involved with others under the pretense that their intentions are towards a relationship only to end up leaving and/or men who ghost others

17   *crackling hopefulness*

The crackling of the fire *feels* hopefulness; or, the fire *feels* hopefulness as it crackles

18   *burning self-pity*

The burning of the fire *feels* self-pity; or, the fire *feels* self-pity as it burns

19 ***One Second Before Midnight (11:59:59 p.m.)***

The title suggests a sense of urgency and possible impending danger due to the countdown to midnight. Midnight, in this context, suggests a period of darkness

20 ***muse***

Philosophy, Spirituality, Human Nature and Love are muses of the speaker of the poem. The speaker of the poem is a poet.

Since the poet's muses are being tortured, the poet is not able to write poetry.

21 ***They should not suffer on account of me***

The muses are being tortured because of the problems and stresses in the poet's life

22 ***bed-hop***

To pass from person to person sexually

23 ***bed-hoppers***

People who pass from person to person sexually

24 ***Courting Field***

An imaginative, spiritual place where lonely, vulnerable hearts go to find other people willing and ready to find love

25 **_Time_**

A poetic personification of time

26 **_Reality_**

A poetic personification of reality

27 **_solar flares_**

Representing bursts of passion

28 **_burning sun_**

In this context, representing a heart filled with passion. Slightly different than the metaphor used in "Cloudy, with Seldom Visits from the Sun" in that the 'sun' in that composition represents the *actions* of the heart whereas in this composition, it represents not only a heart but a heart that loves intensely and thoroughly and greatly

29 **_colonize the Titan Star_**

Representing adequately loving one's heart

30 **_gravity of lovelessness or false love_**

The depressing heaviness that ghosting, toying with one's affections, and cheating weighs upon a person

31 ***weightlessness of interstellar space***

The euphoric feeling that comes when someone loves you and when you love someone

32 ***small town***

In this context, representing a person, a person who is *very* conservative when it comes to casual sex.

33 ***I urbanized myself***

The urbanization of the speaker symbolizes compromising himself, doing what he thought was necessary to attract men. Mainly, becoming more casual with sex.

34 ***city***

In this context, representing a person, a person who is *very* liberal when it comes to casual sex.

35 **French Provincial**

A style of residential architecture

36   *your country*

   Not to be mistaken for one's actual birthplace, this phrase here signifies the limited world of the lover of the speaker of the poem. It represents the lover, their awareness, their immediate world. *See also* **nation**

37   *indigo*

   While used as a name here, whenever indigo is used, in reference to the sky, it means night, nighttime, the night hours

38   *cerulean*

   While used as a name here, whenever cerulean is used, in reference to the sky, it means day, daytime

39   *multicolored, yet visually invisible*

   The fire this phrase refers to is not able to be seen with the naked eye, but due to the honesty of the lover's love, the colorful fire becomes visible. This speaks to the intimacy of the knowledge of the lover. The fire is multicolored because, in this context, the fire of the heart burns varying colors at different times for different things

40   **Weaver**

God. The One believed to have weaved the tapestry of time before time began. When a person dies, it is believed that the Weaver cuts him or her from the tapestry

41   ***tapestry***

A belief that there is a threaded fabric of what has happened, is happening, and will happen, the foresight of which, the Weaver has woven via web and loom

42   ***nation***

Not to be mistaken for one's actual birthplace, this phrase here signifies the limited world of the lover of the speaker of the poem. It represents the lover, their awareness, their immediate world. *See also* ***your country***

43   ***"If This World Were Mine"***

A song originally performed and written by Marvin Gaye, featuring Tammi Terrell. It was covered by Cheryl Lynn and Luther Vandross. In this poetic tale, the Cheryl Lynn and Luther Vandross version should be assumed to be playing

44   ***desert***

Representing the barren landscape of available, *single* men [women or gender non-conforming people]

45 ***Book of Time***

An imaginative, spiritual book that has pre-recorded, archived, and foretold all the history of everything that has happened, is happening, and will happen

46 ***Erykah Badu had taught him well***

Referencing the song "Kiss Me On My Neck" performed by Erykah Badu:

I want somebody to walk up behind me/ And kiss me on my neck/ And breathe on my neck

47 ***salty water***

Tears

48 ***begging others to sustain me***

Depending on others for validation

49 ***wealth gained from my own hard work***

Building my self-esteem by affirming my worth and value with words of affirmation

50 ***experiencing them in and of themselves***

Inspired by Section 192 of Chapter 5 "A Natural History of Morals" of *Beyond Good and Evil* written by Friedrich Nietzsche

51 ***One is really many/At the same time, many are one/One is not one/And many are not many***

    Meant to be a riddle. It means that just as there are multiple states of the firecracker—inert and explosive—there are multiple states, characteristics, moods, talents and so on of human beings. There is this idea among many that people can be defined by one or a few traits, but humans are complex and ever-changing. One person is many things and many of those unique, individual determinants constitute one person

52 ***processed food***

    False doctrine. Heresy. Someone else's "truth". Usually, an erroneous perspective or point of view

53 ***first poem***

    "The Consummation" was not only my first *romantic* poem but it was the first poem I ever wrote

54 ***rain-stained temple***

Symbolizing poetry that was inked in tears

www.ingramcontent.com/pod-product-compliance
Lightning Source LLC
Chambersburg PA
CBHW030432010526
44118CB00011B/598